Mastering Creation
Using
The Law Of Unification

MASTERING CREATION
USING
THE LAW OF UNIFICATION

How To Create New Creations For A New World

THE NEXT STEP ON THE EVOLUTIONARY LADDER OF CONSCIOUSNESS

DIVNEET KAUR LALL

Waterside Productions

Printed in the United States of America

First Printing, 2020

ISBN-13: 978-1-949003-68-0 print edition
ISBN-13: 978-1-949003-69-7 ebook edition

Waterside Productions
2055 Oxford Ave
Cardiff, CA 92007
www.waterside.com

*THE WORK IS REVERENTLY
DEDICATED TO THE GURU
AND CREATORS*

"Ik Onkar"[1]

Sri Guru Granth Sahib Ji

Translation: "The Creator Is In The Creation
And Yet Is Beyond The Creation; The
Creator And The Creation Are One"

Table of Contents

Preface

As a child, I was very fond of books. I used to read books because I thought they could provide me the answers to the questions that kept occuring in my mind. Although as time passed, I realized that answers to the questions that a man keeps asking cannot be found in books. And books can only point toward the direction or path following which the questions are dissolved and a state of fulfillment is achieved. But before this realization, my inner self kept searching for something that it could not find in worldly pleasures. The comforts of the world were unable to satisfy my deeper urge—the urge to know the truth of creation.

I distinctly remember sitting on a wooden chair and holding onto an old book when I was 10. It was the first book, that I felt, contained all the answers to my budding curiosity as a young kid. I read the book word by word and practiced all the instructions provided in the book. I cannot recall the name of the book or the author, but I still remember some practices that helped me develop an understanding of the human mind. The urge to know the truth of creation also made me practice meditation and yoga during teenage. These practices and knowledge helped me gain an understanding of the human form and thus satisfy my urge to some extent. However, the understanding I gained was conceptual and the experiences were momentary. Steadily, working with the practices and knowledge, I reached a point where the practices stopped working and the knowledge ceased to make sense. Everything from the outside stopped working because something from the inside started working. The ideas about my path started coming from a place that I did not know even existed. I had no other option but to follow the ideas that were striking me with full force. These ideas led to the creation of "Mastering Creation Using The Law Of Unification."

> "Mastering Creation Using The Law Of Unification" came into existence to help man establish new and higher levels of consciousness on the planet and to make him the creator of new creations.

– Divneet Kaur Lall
New Delhi, India

Acknowledgments

The book would not have reached the readers without the trust of Mr. Bill Gladstone in the work. Mr. Gladstone's contribution to the work has been heartwarming. I sincerely thank Mr. Bill Gladstone for his support and guidance that led me through the uncharted territory of the publishing world gracefully and effortlessly.

Introduction

Today, we are witnessing a tremendous increase in depressive and anxious states among men. Several people are finding themselves trapped in their lives, and this is adversely affecting their mental health. There were never so many mental health providers in the world as there are now. Man's dependency on external sources for stabilizing his mind is increasing steeply. Man is sufficiently capable of taking care of his mind, but he is unaware of the factor that is causing the mental turmoil inside the humans everywhere around the world.

Mental health specialists typically work with the experiences of man and suggest methods for producing different experiences for him. The subconscious mind is considered vital in helping man liberate himself of suffering. The methods of changing the thoughts and experiences by using the subconscious mind may seem to provide satisfactory results by producing changed habits and thoughts in a man. However, these methods cannot provide the deep fulfillment necessary for the man to completely negate his suffering. Man's suffering cannot be eradicated by mechanically changing the thoughts or experiences. This is because the depressive states although are experienced in the human mind and anxious sensations are felt in the human body, the cause of these states cannot be perceived through the human mind or senses. Further, until the cause remains unknown, the state of suffering cannot be alleviated.

Another well-known method that is believed to cure man's suffering is spirituality. However, man is often reluctant to follow the path of spirituality as it seems to lack the worldly element in it. Further, even if someone takes this path, it is not long before he is compelled by certain forces to leave it altogether and fulfill his worldly duties. Therefore, to help man overcome his suffering and provide him the best of both the worlds—the spiritual and the material, "Mastering Creation Using The Law Of Unification" opens a new path that leads man to evolved levels of consciousness. Man can use these evolved levels to become a creator of new creations that can evolve the planet and of new life free of suffering.

By diving deep into the minds of geniuses, "Mastering Creation Using The Law Of Unification" explores the hidden knowledge underlying the motifs found in ancient mythologies and makes the formula of creation available for man to use. The formula of creation can be used to master the process of creation and to become a creator of a new life and new creations. This formula will help man and the planet to attain evolved levels of consciousness and to eradicate suffering and distortion. "Mastering Creation Using The Law Of Unification" discusses the theory of creation and the law followed by the creators and geniuses. However, the purpose of the book is not to burden the human mind with more concepts or theories, instead to open a new path that, if taken, can simplify life and make man the creator of new creations. Further, "Mastering Creation Using The Law Of Unification" unifies the theories and laws of creation and provides a "unified law" that consists the essence of all laws of creation. This "unified law" when followed provides man a new perception that is necessary for living a fulfilling life.

For the convenience of the readers, the book is divided into two parts. The first part consists the theory that discusses the causes of suffering and distortion, the path of creators, and the law followed by them. The second part details out a step-by-step guide to practice the law followed by the creators. The readers should first read the first part of the book in order to attain a proper understanding of the path of creators before proceeding to the practices provided in the second part of the book. Only after understanding the theory, will the readers be able to practice the law with utmost efficiency and can avoid any pitfalls on the path of creation.

While reading, the readers will observe that I have used the words "consciousness," "new consciousness," and "higher consciousness" interchangeably when referring to evolving consciousness. This is to make readers aware of the unpredictability of the ever-flowing and ever-evolving consciousness that does not take any shape and that cannot be described through a single word. The readers will also come across some solitary words such as "whole" and "new" that have a broader reference in the book and will be easily grasped once the theory is understood. Moreover, I have used the word "man" to refer to humans. This does not indicate my preference towards a certain gender. But, while writing the book, "man" came out more naturally with the flow of the text. So, I did not make an effort to change it to any other word and interrupt the flow of consciousness. The readers are free to change the words in the text, if it allows them to more conveniently grasp the essence of the work.

To understand the cause of distortion and suffering, man needs to recognize the ways of consciousness. A distortion is always experienced in the outer world or in the inner mental world of the human form because of the resistance of forms against the movements of consciousness. Consciousness operates and evolves through forms. Mental turmoil, anxiety, depression, and suffering are results of unconscious prevention of evolution that has to occur in one's life and on the planet. Unless man realizes that he must release the old in order to allow the new consciousness to work and blossom his existence, the depressive and anxious states will prevail. The change required for a man, as a medicine for his suffering, cannot be implemented using the limited knowledge of the human mind. It can only be accomplished through higher levels of consciousness that can help in creating new creations for the evolution of man and the planet.

Consciousness desires to evolve through the human form, and in the process, wants man to create new models and frameworks that are as evolved as the new consciousness. "Mastering Creation Using The Law Of Unification" has been created to aid the smooth working of the process of evolution by making man aware of the evolving consciousness which can be used to create new frameworks and provide him a fulfilling and evolved existence. It is created using the same law that is discussed in it. The law has helped creators bring their creations into existence for evolution and will further help all those who choose the path of "Mastering Creation."

Mastering Creation
Using
The Law Of Unification

Part I

The Theory And Unification

"Companions, the creator seeketh, not corpses—and not herds or believers either. Fellow-creators the creator seeketh—those who grave new values on new tables. Companions, the creator seeketh, and fellow-reapers: for everything is ripe for the harvest with him."[2]

Friedrich Nietzsche

Chapter ~ 1
Evolving Consciousness

Consciousness

In the universe, man or any other species exists with the sole purpose of working in accordance with the consciousness that gives form to it, moves it, and evolves through it. When consciousness evolves in a form, the form through which it evolves also undergoes evolution. Consciousness also creates new forms when it desires to evolve. Consciousness does not announce before beginning the evolution process nor does it allow anyone to interfere with this process. If consciousness enjoys the evolution process, so does the form through which the process is being accomplished, but there should be no resistance in the form toward evolution. In the world of form, consciousness attains its growth through forms.

Consciousness is everywhere. It acts through all that moves or grows. It is the guiding principle underlying the actions of a man, and it is responsible for the movements of all forms present in the universe. Consciousness is all that is, yet, humans or any other forms cannot perceive it with their senses. Consciousness has been evolving on this planet since it first created water, land, and vegetation in the world of form; it then brought the animal kingdom to the planet, followed by the human form. Across all the forms created by consciousness, the human form is the most evolved. This form is capable of attaining higher and more evolved levels of consciousness. This is a privilege available only to man and not provided to the other forms created by consciousness. The human form, therefore, is a medium through which consciousness can advance its evolution and the evolution of the whole—humans, the planet, and the universe—by creating new evolved frameworks and models that can support new higher levels of ever-evolving consciousness.

When consciousness evolves in a form, it begins to spread the effects of new and evolved consciousness upon other forms located around it. Consequently, either the consciousness in the other forms also evolves, or the forms, owing to resistance, obstruct the evolution of consciousness within them. The frameworks, structures, or models that form the basis of a society or civilization established in a region of evolved consciousness also encounter the effects of the evolving consciousness. If these frameworks, structures, or models are too old and outdated to hold and support the evolving consciousness, then they must be recreated to support the new higher levels of consciousness; otherwise, they may begin to collapse, as they are not created around the evolved consciousness of the region. When the society or civilization is reluctant toward the creation of new frameworks, structures, or models that can hold the new evolved consciousness and stubbornly attempts to cling to the old frameworks, the new consciousness exerts pressure. This pressure is experienced in the world of form as anxiety, suffering, or destruction. The suffering experienced on the planet is not to punish man, but to make him aware of the higher levels of consciousness available for his growth and evolution. Man can use these higher levels of consciousness to create the new according to the new evolved consciousness for the growth and evolution of the planet.

While the higher evolved levels of consciousness are available for man's growth, he still has a choice. The choice available is to update the old models and frameworks and become the creator of the new, which can be created using the new higher levels of consciousness, or get dragged along with the evolving consciousness on the way toward evolution, while consciousness accomplishes its goals. When consciousness desires to evolve the planet, evolution cannot be prevented. If man tries to obstruct evolution, he will only suffer. Thus, the conscious choice of becoming the creator and mastering the process of creation can lead man to new heights and new levels of consciousness, while consciousness will take care of his existence, needs, and life on the planet.

Levels of Consciousness

The forms created by consciousness operate at varying levels of consciousness. The forms that are unaware of their experiences or their actions operate at lower levels of consciousness. For example, an insect may bite someone, but it will do so out of impulse or habit as it is not aware that it is biting. Similarly, when the human form works under the influence of its habits and conditioning, it operates at lower levels of consciousness. The more man becomes aware of his actions and experiences, the less habits and conditioning control him. Thus, he is able to work at higher levels of consciousness. With a decrease in awareness, man's attention is drawn into the incessant streams of thoughts, leading to entrapment of man in the patterns of performing unconscious actions. The level of consciousness around which the human form works is highly related to the states of joy and fulfillment that the form experiences. When the level of consciousness increases in a human form or around the human form, the same experiences that appear dissatisfactory and empty around a lower level of consciousness become more joyful and lighthearted.

Consciousness can evolve with an increase in the awareness of the forms. Therefore, various factors can result in the availability of higher levels of consciousness on the planet. This availability could occur because of the newborns with evolved minds who bring new consciousness to the planet, because of the ones who awaken and realize the truth, or because of ones who gradually become more aware as they move through their lives. With an increase in the level of consciousness, it becomes easier to move in accordance with the movements of the evolving consciousness and clearly perceive its role in the functioning of the whole. Therefore, of all the forms present on the planet, working with the human form, which works around higher levels of consciousness in comparison to other forms, is easier for the evolving consciousness; this also helps consciousness to maintain the functioning of the whole and accomplish its further evolution. The whole system works perfectly when everything in the universe functions in accordance with the consciousness. Moreover, a single element in the whole that resists the movement of the consciousness brings suffering not only upon itself but also for the whole. All that the consciousness requires is the cooperation of its created forms in order to maintain the smooth functioning of the whole.

The thoughts or emotions experienced by a human form cannot help in determining the level of the consciousness around which the form works. This is because consciousness is the "awareness" of the thoughts and emotions. Therefore, thoughts and emotions of man are not responsible for raising or lowering the level of consciousness in man. Furthermore, levels of consciousness cannot be switched by altering the thoughts and emotions experienced in the human form. Positive thoughts do not necessarily help man attain higher states of consciousness, and similarly, negative thoughts do not make him reach lower levels of consciousness. Thoughts can change feelings in the human form, and feelings can affect the thoughts originating within the human mind. Thus, happy thoughts generate feelings of happiness, and similarly, feelings of nervousness can generate fearful thoughts. However, thoughts and feelings cannot make a man work around a higher level of consciousness and thus experience joy or make him work around a lower level of consciousness and experience dullness and dissatisfaction. Therefore, the level of consciousness operating in a form can only be determined by its awareness level.

The thoughts and actions that originate in the human form in an unconscious state of mind lack awareness and occur because of the conditioning stored in the plane of the subconscious mind of man. Moreover, as these actions originate without man's awareness, it can be concluded that the subconscious plane exists at a lower level of consciousness. It is generally believed that a man who can change the thoughts originating from the subconscious plane can also change his external circumstances. The use of the subconscious plane of the mind is popular in psychotherapy. The subconscious mind, in psychotherapy, is used to identify hidden triggers underlying certain behavioral patterns in man and to change the conditioning that operates in someone's life and produces undesirable experiences. The subconscious mind is a wide plane of collective information of the whole human consciousness. However, all this information is not accompanied with the awareness found in the planes of higher levels of consciousness. Thus, using the subconscious plane to change life for better experiences does not ensure joy and fulfillment associated with higher levels of consciousness. In addition, the ideas present in the subconscious plane come from lower levels of consciousness and are not the "evolved" ideas that can provide new solutions to the problems of the conscious plane of existence in which man lives.

The subconscious plane can be accessed easily when man is under the influence of external substance or external will power that is able to cease or control the functioning of his conscious mind. For example, man is unable to use his conscious mind under the influence of alcohol, and on several occasions, he regrets his actions performed under such influence. These actions originate from the subconscious plane, which he enters when his conscious mind stops functioning. Any external influence used to stop the functioning of the conscious mind makes man less conscious, and he thus steps on the lower level of consciousness where the subconscious plane exists. Suggestion is another form of external influence that is used to forcefully put ideas in the subconscious mind of man. Hypnotism, psychotherapy, drugs, medicines, and other influencers are used to change or receive ideas from the subconscious mind. The plane of the subconscious mind has its own place when man wants to make alterations in his conditionings, but changes in the lower planes of consciousness will not help man in attaining the evolved levels of consciousness and experiencing the state of joy.

In the domains of human psychology, there are methods for relieving man of his old conditioning and forming new habits or beliefs as a cure to the suffering or pain. However, even after following all these procedures, sometimes, it may become difficult to get rid of the old conditioning or thoughts. Also, even if one does get rid of the old conditioning, the new conditioning does not help in providing relief from the suffering that he experiences because when he replaces the old conditioning with new ideas, these new ideas arise from the same lower levels of consciousness from where the old ideas originated. In order to eradicate the suffering of man, the new ideas need to originate from the planes of evolved levels of consciousness, which can help him in his growth and evolution.

❧

Need to Evolve

Evolution of forms means improving the quality of the forms that consciousness produced earlier, to establish new and higher levels of consciousness on the planet and to help in the growth of already existing forms. The evolution is the force of consciousness that urges existing forms to aspire for higher levels of existence. Evolution begins in the forms when the consciousness perceives a need for a new and evolved existence to be brought into the world. This results in substantial changes being brought by the higher consciousness in the existing structures, frameworks, and forms. These changes can occur gradually over a period if the evolution is not interrupted or hindered by the old forms and can produce new forms and frameworks. However, if the evolution is interrupted, then the changes may come upon acutely and dreadfully. This occurs when old forms resist the new.

Consciousness generates a need for evolution in the forms when it recognizes the older forms' great suffering in order to minimize or eradicate this suffering through the creation of the new frameworks and structures. When the forms overlook the need for evolution because of their fear of transition or because of their inability to recognize it, then the suffering aggravates until new frameworks and models are created as desired by the new evolved levels of consciousness. The work of consciousness is to maintain the proper functioning of the whole through the process of evolution, whenever it is required. Suffering in the forms only occurs when they resist the movements of consciousness and, as a result, try to obstruct it from fulfilling its work.

In order to evolve, the consciousness provided "mind" to the human form which if used efficiently can help it to reach the highest levels of consciousness. The mind that understands its role in the process of evolution creates new creations, when guided by the evolving consciousness. The mind that does not understands its role remains entangled in its troubles and is unable to aid the process of evolution. There are several instances when man has utilized his mind to its highest potential and has developed new creations for the growth of the planet and evolution of the whole. Today, man finds himself trapped in the web of his mind' entanglements that are resulted by an overload of information and limited reasoning. With increased access to information, these entanglements have become so enormous that they obstruct man's path of evolution. When a mind overpowered by entanglements builds something, it builds around the lower levels of consciousness. The forms that are built around lower levels of consciousness do not aid in the evolution of the planet. Therefore, in order to overcome these entanglements and prevent it from establishing lower levels of consciousness on the planet through its produced forms, man is required to create the new forms according to the guidance of higher levels of consciousness and not of the limited domains of knowledge and information of mind. The guidance of higher consciousness is necessary to evolve and create forms that can bring joy and fulfillment to man and to the planet.

The entanglements of the mind keep the human form bound to the old, thus preventing his evolution and growth. More the entanglements, more is the effort required to give up the old and move toward the new. The evolution of forms guided by the evolving consciousness frees them from the entanglements of the mind and provides them with a new perspective required for new creations. The mind entrapped in these entanglements attempts to control and dictate the movements of the consciousness so that it does not have to leave the familiar. The fear of leaving the familiar entraps the mind in its own entanglements. When such a stage arrives, the consciousness is required to intervene forcibly and carry out the evolution to bring the new forms into existence. The task of the human mind is to follow the directions of higher consciousness, if it has to efficiently fulfill its role in the process of evolution and free itself from its own entanglements.

❧

Working with Higher Consciousness

As the consciousness evolves inside the forms, it amplifies the evolution by bringing the effects of the new evolved consciousness in the outside world through the process of creation—the creation of new lives or new forms and frameworks. Thus, even when man fulfills the process of evolution of consciousness within, the work is not completed. The consciousness urges him to bring higher levels of evolved consciousness in the world of form by creating new creations for the evolution of the planet. Following the path of fulfillment of desires of higher consciousness is a way through which the creators help advance the process of evolution in the world of form.

Often, the consciousness brings with it experiences that appear difficult to a man, but as the work of consciousness unfolds, the same experiences start to seem as a necessary link in the chain of evolution of the whole. Therefore, the new experiences that are presented to a man when the process of evolution occurs must not be feared. Fear can cause a man to reject the new while trying to retain the old and the familiar. Clinging to the evolving consciousness and working according to its directions is the only well-ordered path for man's evolution and growth. As the human mind gets burdened with tons of information coming from several directions, it becomes hard to choose the right path for its growth and evolution. When man learns to move forward according to the higher consciousness, he does not have to choose anymore and becomes the creator of a new life and walks the path of evolution effortlessly.

Most of man's suffering is the result of his resistance toward the works that the higher consciousness wants to accomplish through him because he is unable to differentiate between the works influenced by the higher levels of consciousness and the ones originating from the lower levels of consciousness. Often times, if man is informed that he needs to work with the higher consciousness to evolve, he would start fantasizing the works which the consciousness may want him to do in order to evolve. But the works of the new consciousness do not fit in with the expectations of man. So, a man must give away the expectations and be like a blank sheet of paper while the higher consciousness guides him in the creation of the new.

Man is required to learn to differentiate the works of the higher consciousness from the works influenced by the lower levels of consciousness to become the creator of the new. It can be achieved when he becomes more aware of his thoughts and feelings. As discussed earlier, consciousness is the awareness of thoughts, emotions, or actions. When the awareness increases, the level of consciousness around which man starts working also increases. If a man can become more aware of his thoughts, emotions, and actions, he can work around a higher level of consciousness. It then gets easier for him to differentiate between the works influenced by the higher levels of consciousness and those by the lower levels of consciousness. Consciousness has laid down a unique path for every form for its evolution. To walk on this unique path, the forms need to discard the information and knowledge that oppose the path which consciousness wants him to move toward. Working with the higher consciousness is the only way out of suffering and into the freedom, trust, and growth of oneself and of the whole.

An essential element of the evolution process is to work with the evolving consciousness. The human mind is too cluttered with thoughts and information because of which there is no space for the new to emerge. The consciousness brings the required space for the emergence of the new through which the evolution can be accomplished. This space also provides a new perception to man to clearly understand the functioning of consciousness and the role of human mind in the evolution of the whole. Without this recognition, man finds it difficult to work with higher consciousness. The creators are guided by the higher levels of understanding of the existence and of life. They are not born as creators, but they consciously choose to become creators by working with the higher levels of consciousness. Thus, the process of creation and evolution is open to all those who are ready for this wonderful adventure of life and living up to their highest potential.

> "Verily, verily, I say unto you, He that believeth on me, the works that I do shall he do also; and greater works than these shall he do; because I go unto my Father."[3]
>
> King James Version

Chapter - 2
Theory of Creation

Creators

Creators challenge the existing frameworks and models present in the society and provide the world with new forms and frameworks, which portray the new evolved levels of consciousness. The desire that urges the creators to create new creations is not the desire of the creators, but it is the desire of the evolving consciousness that wants to evolve the whole through the creations of the creators. The works of the creators do not benefit only them, but every human form that evolves and reaches higher levels of consciousness through their works. The creators conquer their minds to create new forms and frameworks, which can help others to conquer their lives. Creators can be found everywhere; they can be seen in the humblest of places hidden away from the eyes of the public so that they can concentrate their energy upon their work. They can also be found in the most opulent places, or working amidst the people while guiding them on their path to freedom and evolution. Creators have always been on the planet for the service of the whole to bring the new from the higher levels of consciousness. They establish the higher levels of consciousness on the planet by creating new creations.

Creators leave their imprint because the paths they follow are unique and new. No matter how trivial their paths may seem to others, their lives immensely contribute to maintaining the functioning of the whole and to aiding in the evolution of the whole. By living their lives according to the higher consciousness and following their unique paths, the creators fulfill the highest purpose of their existence and add to the evolution of the planet. In order to be a creator, it is not a necessity to create something extraordinary, although that can also be achieved if the consciousness desires. But creation is more about the creation of a new life or a new framework or model, which is a unique expression of the higher consciousness operating through a unique human form.

Numerous names appear in the mind when man thinks about the creators who have contributed to the evolution of the planet. Although each creator seems distinctive from the other, their chosen field of work, that is, "To Create" and their purpose, that is, "To Evolve," is always the same. This is because their desire belongs to the same higher consciousness that works through all the creators. Creators plunge into the mysterious to bring new solutions to the problems of the world. While working on their creation, they do not worry about losing the old. They follow their unique paths toward the new creations without heeding to any doubt about their work or path.

Creation is a process that has been carried out since ages. There have been Gods and Deities, in the history of man, who are known as the creators of the cosmos. The universe came into existence through a process of creation. Creation is the basis of every existence on the planet, and the secrets of the process of creation have been shared with man many times using stories, symbols, and anecdotes by the ancients. They have always been available to man to be used by him for his evolution and growth. The need to evolve and to live at a higher level of existence thus can be acted upon by first understanding the theory of creation. Following which, it can be used to accomplish the task of creation of the new in order to evolve.

∞

Creator Gods and Deities

According to mythology, in order to maintain the proper functioning of the cosmos, various Gods and Goddesses were allocated different duties and tasks of the universe. All the Gods and Deities of ancient mythology have been used as figurative expressions to explain the laws governing the functions of the universe. Although mythology seems impractical from the perspective of science, it is based upon the laws of the universe which, if understood and utilized properly, are able to provide man the solutions and answers to all his problems and questions, respectively. The stories and characters of ancient mythologies are not to be believed or worshipped, but to be questioned, interpreted, understood, and used to recognize the role of man in the steady functioning of the world. As man has not grasped the concepts and laws provided through the stories and characters of ancient mythologies and is not able to use them in his life, the world today is suffering and distorting.

The creation is the function of the universe managed by the Creator Gods and Deities. Therefore, the Gods and Deities of mythology who were considered the creators hold the key to unlock the truth of the process of creation. They have always followed a law to accomplish the process of creation. This law can be known by closely observing the Creator Gods and Deities of different ancient mythologies, which are depicted in a similar manner—as a combination of a serpent and a pair of wings. A feathered serpent, named Quetzalcoatl[4], has been the most important deity in the mythology of Mesoamerica, known as a boundary-maker between the earth and the sky and also considered a creator deity in the Mesoamerican culture. Similarly, another deity named Isis[5], the Egyptian goddess, was worshipped as a Creator God and is depicted with a pair of wings, wearing a crown that holds a hawk and a cobra. This combination of the serpent and wings portrayed in these mythological Creator Gods and Deities provides the information about the law followed by the Creator

Gods. By understanding the law, it is possible for man to master the process of creation as the Creator Gods did. Man can, thus, use the law for his evolution and growth.

As it is already known, the serpent crawls on the plane of the earth, or it moves in water, and the birds with the help of the wings fly in the plane of the sky. Therefore, the figures of the Creator Gods and Deities demonstrate the merger of the two planes by using the combination of serpent and wings in their figures. These figures guide man about the law, which is followed by the creators to accomplish the work of creation for the smooth functioning of the universe. Comprehending it further, it can be said that when the powers of the two planes are combined together, it results in the creation of the new. The Creator Gods and Deities of mythology provide man with the knowledge on the workings of the process of creation. This unspoken truth of the creative powers hidden in each individual can be harnessed by implementing a law. This information on the law has been provided to us by our ancestors using symbols. Symbols can explain far more elaborately than words; therefore, the ancients have always used them to provide information about various truths. But, with the increased use of language and words, man is now capable enough to understand and describe the truths of creation by using words creatively.

The plane represented by the serpent, where the serpent crawls, is a plane of matter that has structure and boundaries. The plane represented by the wings is a plane that is powered by freedom and limitlessness, similar to that experienced by birds when they fly. Therefore, the figures of the Creator Gods and Deities give as much importance to freedom and limitlessness as to structure and boundaries in the process of creation. Structure and boundaries are found in the plane of human mind. Thus, there exists another plane comprising the qualities of limitlessness and freedom, which plays an important role in the process of creation. The figures of the Creator Gods and Deities show the merger of the two planes to explain the process of creation. A similar type of merger can also be observed within the minds of the geniuses when they create new creations in the world.

Geniuses and Their Minds

Geniuses are the creators who first understood the law through which the new creations can be brought into existence and then followed it conscientiously to create new creations. The man has been attempting to figure out the secrets of the genius mind, either in the lumps of the brains of geniuses or through constructing intelligence tests. But the power of the genius cannot be found in the chunks of matter or in the intelligence of the brain. Instead, the power of a genius mind can only be discovered by understanding the law that the geniuses followed to create the new creations. Throughout history, they have confirmed that their creations were not created by their mind, rather they came across the idea either in a dream or in a vision when their minds were relaxed for a microsecond. The ideas occurring through dreams or visions are a well-known scenario to man, as many of the greatest inventors in history have created their masterpiece by giving form to the ideas that occurred through their dreams or visions.

Srinivasa Ramanujan has discussed his mathematical dreams, and Elias Howe figured out how to create the modern lockstitch sewing machine by an idea of a hole in the tip seen in his dream. August Kekulé, who was a German organic chemist known for the discovery of the benzene ring, dreamt of his new ideas through visions. Talking about his dream in which he received an idea, he said, "I was sitting writing at my textbook but the work did not progress; my thoughts were elsewhere. I turned my chair to the fire and dozed. Again the atoms were gamboling before my eyes. This time the smaller groups kept modestly in the background. My mental eye, rendered more acute by the repeated visions of the kind, could now distinguish larger structures of manifold conformation: long rows, sometimes more closely fitted together; all twining and twisting in a snake-like motion. But look! What was that? One of the snakes had seized hold of its own tail, and the form whirled mockingly before my eyes. As if by a flash of lightning I awoke; and this time also I spent the rest of the night in working out the rest of the hypothesis."[6] August Kekulé received the idea for the benzene ring when his mind was relaxed, which means the idea was not received from the plane of his mind. For the readers' convenience, let's refer to this another plane through which the ideas are received as the plane of the idea mind.

Kekulé further said, "Let us learn to dream, gentlemen, then perhaps we shall find the truth. But let us beware of publishing our dreams before they have been put to the proof by the waking understanding."[7] This statement shows that the geniuses pay as much importance to the waking understanding as they do to the ideas presented through dreams. This is similar to the Creator Gods and Deities who give as much importance to freedom and limitlessness as to structure and boundaries in the process of creation. The geniuses too demonstrate the merger of the two planes—"ideas" and "waking understanding." The plane through which the dreams or visions are presented is the plane of the idea mind, and the plane of waking understanding is the plane of the human mind. The geniuses receive the ideas for their creations from the plane of the idea mind and use the plane of the mind to give form to those ideas. Thus, it can be concluded that both the Creator Gods and Deities and the geniuses follow the same law and combine the powers of the planes of the idea mind and the mind for new creations.

The creators never credit their creations to their minds because they are aware that the idea they worked upon originated from a plane other than the plane of the mind. Once the idea is presented to the creators, their mind starts working on it in order to turn the idea into a new creation. The idea has the power to awaken the dormant parts of the human mind so that it can be realized to its full potential by using the unique expression of the creator. The new ideas approach man from the plane of the idea mind. They either approach him through dreams, visions or subtle understanding. These ideas can be used by man to live a fulfilling life and for his evolution.

Fight of Eagle and Serpent

Another evidence of the theory of creation that provides further elaboration of the same law followed by the Creator Gods and Deities and the geniuses is provided by the motif of the famous fight between the eagle and the serpent found in various myths. A statue that dates back to 50–150 CE of an eagle fighting with a serpent is kept in the Cincinnati Art Museum of Ohio, USA taken from the Nabataean Temple, Khirbet et-Tannur in Jordan. This fight is also a part of the Etana myth and can be found on the Babylonian seal of the third millenium BC.[8] Similar kinds of statues, myths, and motifs are found in various parts of the world.

Man has developed different interpretations around the motif of the fight. Some consider the eagle to be a symbol of the "good" and the serpent to be a symbol of the "evil." Others assume that the eagle–serpent may point to the light–shadow aspects of duality. Relating these symbols to the concept of duality may provide some explanation, but it does not provide a complete clarity regarding the meaning of this fight discovered throughout ancient mythologies of the world. In addition, mythologies depict the eagle and serpent fighting with each other, and alternatively, the images of the Creator Gods and Deities show a combination of eagle/ wings and serpent/snake in their figures, as if they have reconciled after the fight.

The fight between the eagle and the snake does not necessarily represents a fight of the good and the evil, where eagle depicts good and serpent represents evil. This is because good is a cause of creation and evil is a cause of destruction in the world of form. But the Creator Gods who are known for creation are represented using a combination of both the eagle/wings and the serpent/snake. Thus, the fight between the eagle and the serpent has a much deeper meaning in the theory of creation and must not be interpreted simply as a symbol of good–evil, or light–shadow duality. It provides to man the information which he can use to become the creator of his life and attain fulfillment and growth through the process of creation. Another perception of the fight between the eagle and serpent and the images of the Creator Gods and Deities of the ancient mythology, where the eagle and serpent are found together as "one" can be that the purpose of the fight is not to kill or destroy the other contender but to achieve an agreement between both the parties so that their powers can be used together in the process of creation. The reconciliation of the eagle and serpent seen in the images of the Creator Gods and Deities of ancient mythology is the portrayal of the agreement between the plane of the idea mind and the plane of the mind.

As the eagles fly at a higher level than at which the serpent crawls, the higher consciousness works through the plane of the idea mind symbolized by the eagle/ wings. Therefore, the fight between the eagle and the serpent represents the fight between the higher consciousness and the plane of the human mind, which occurs when the human mind rejects the new ideas provided to him through the plane of the idea mind for his evolution, because of the influence of the lower levels of consciousness. This hinders the evolution, creating more suffering for man. The eagle represents the higher consciousness that wants to work with the plane of the human mind represented by the serpent for the creation of the new. When the eagle and serpent come together and work in unison, they become the creators represented by the combination of the wings of the eagle and the serpent in the figures of Creator Gods and Deities of ancient mythology. In these figures, the wings represent the plane of the idea mind through which the higher consciousness provides the new ideas, and the serpent represents the plane of the mind that gives form to the ideas.

Further, the fight between the eagle and the serpent also symbolizes the struggle faced by man when he resists the movements of the higher consciousness. It occurs when lower levels of consciousness act as hindrance when higher consciousness provides ideas for the manifestation of new creations and evolution. As the higher consciousness provides the ideas through the idea mind, represented by the eagle, and the mind manifests it in form, which is represented by the serpent, the images of the Creator Gods show that they have managed to unify the powers of both the idea mind and the mind and have become the creators of the new.

Tree of Life

The archetype of the Tree of Life cannot be forgotten while talking about the theory of creation. Various religions and mythologies in history have mentioned the Tree of Life as the sacred tree. Although a lot of interpretations are available according to the various perceptions, the Tree of Life is an allegory used to describe the Creator—the one who brings the new creations of the higher consciousness to the world. A tree bears fruits with the help of roots, trunk, and branches. The roots of the tree provide nutrients, and trunk and branches help to produce the fruits. Similarly, creators who bring creations into existence do so with the help of the plane of the idea mind and the plane of the mind. Here, the plane of the idea mind provides ideas and the plane of the mind helps in the creation of the new forms. The creator gives life to the new ideas; therefore, a creator is a Tree of Life.

Figure 1.
Yggdrasil (also called Tree of Life)
As depicted in English translation of the Prose
Edda, 1847 Painted by Oluf Olufsen Bagge

In the Bhagavad Gita, there is a reference to the tree of life called aśhvatth[9], which has its roots upwards and the branches downwards. This inverted Tree of Life conveys that the roots or the idea mind is at a higher level than the branches or the mind. Therefore, the higher levels of consciousness work through the plane of the idea mind. The Tree of Life explains the same law represented by the images of the Creator Gods and Deities and also by the minds of the geniuses.

Although root is the hidden part of a tree, it is the source of provision for the tree to produce fruits. Similarly, the idea mind, which remains hidden from man, is the source of ideas for the creation of his life and the creation of the new. The trunk and branches of the tree are media through which the provision transfers and fruits are brought into this world. Similarly, the plane of mind acts as a medium to bring the ideas into existence by giving them form in the world. Unless the roots and the trunk of the tree work together, the fruits cannot be produced. So, the creations can only come into existence when the powers of the idea mind work in cooperation with the powers of the mind.

The Bhagavad Gita also talks about man's attachment to the fruits because of which he is unable to connect with the source of provision and, thus, hinders his own evolution. The creators remain unattached to the results of their works. Therefore, while following the law and walking on the path of mastering creation, they do not get attached to the fruits, or they would lose the connection with the source. The Tree of Life is a metaphor used in all ancient religions to explain the process of creation. The whole universe came into existence when the powers of the idea mind combined with the powers of the mind. This law is the basis for each creation in the world.

> "Verily He is the Tree of Life, that bringeth forth the fruits of God, the Exalted, the Powerful, the Great."[10]
>
> Bahá'í Prayers

Chapter - 3
Law of Unification

Individual Dharma

In its true essence, the word "Dharma" popularly known as religion means the "Law." It is not a law constructed by the society or the world, but by the higher consciousness, which governs the working of the whole universe. By defining Dharma as religion, man has confined it to an adherence to religious codes. But, the higher "Law", which is the actual Dharma, cannot be followed by simply adhering to religious regulations. Also, man cannot realize the Dharma that exists for his evolution and fulfillment solely by gaining a conceptual understanding of these rules. The higher law is individual to every human form, and it is the duty of man to follow his unique Dharma. Thus, Dharma can also be referred to as the "Individual Duty" or the "Individual Dharma," bestowed upon man by the higher consciousness for his evolution, growth, and fulfillment, and also for the evolution of the whole.

To adhere to several rules and principles set by man and live one's life according to them is a tedious act. It also causes a state of confusion and doubt in man regarding the basis of these regulations. A man's already complicated life will become even more complicated if he attempts to understand and follow every law that governs the universe and its functioning. Therefore, the higher consciousness sets an Individual Dharma for every man. There is no need for man to follow several laws of the universe to ensure a fulfilling life if he follows the Individual Dharma. The pitfalls involved in blindly following these laws of the universe are also eliminated by following one's Individual Dharma. Such a risk arises when an individual follows the laws of the universe for the fulfillment of the desires of the lower levels of consciousness. In this case, the laws may work but will not aid in evolution and growth of man. In addition, this will take him further away from the higher consciousness because of which, in the near future, he will find himself unable to move forward in his life.

It is difficult for a man to learn to follow all the laws of the universe and use them precisely and accurately without making mistakes. Therefore, to simplify his life, the higher consciousness has provided each individual with his Individual Dharma. It can be followed using the law used by the creators for the purpose of creation. As discussed in the previous chapter, the creators follow a law supported by the higher consciousness, which is demonstrated by the merger of two planes, called the "Law Of Unification." By following the Law of Unification, unifying the powers of the idea mind with the powers of the mind, the creators fulfill their Individual Dharma and bring forth new creations into the universe. The higher consciousness ensures that the Absolute Dharma, the Dharma of the whole, is followed with utmost perfection while each individual follows his Individual Dharma. Man's unique Dharma gives him the power to be the creator of his life under the supervision of the higher consciousness. Thus, man creates new forms and structures to support the evolution of the whole.

The influence of the lower levels of consciousness often obstructs man from fulfilling his Individual Dharma. Being unaware of these influences, he blindly follows the desires originating from the lower levels of consciousness and squanders his life fulfilling these desires instead of his Individual Dharma. This choice of fulfilling his Individual Dharma is conferred to man. The works of the lower levels of consciousness can never provide man the fulfillment attained by working on his Individual Dharma under the guidance of the higher consciousness. Rising above these influences and following the Law of Unification is the only path that can take man closer to his evolution and make him a creator of his life and of the new, which can be created through him.

Law of Unification

The Law of Unification followed by the Creator Gods and Deities and the geniuses can be stated as follows:

when the powers of the plane of the mind overcome the forces of the lower levels of consciousness and work in cooperation with the powers of the plane of the idea mind, it results in the unification of both the planes and thus causes evolution and creation of the new.

The powers of the plane of mind or the plane of idea mind are insufficient when used individually to carry out the process of creation. Only when both the idea mind and the mind work together, the creations are brought into existence. Without the powers of the mind, the idea mind cannot give form to the ideas, and without the powers of the idea mind, the mind cannot fulfill the Individual Dharma and complete the process of creation. This unification can be achieved only when the mind overcomes the forces of the lower consciousness that try to hinder it. The forces approach the human mind from the planes of lower levels of consciousness and work against the unification of the plane of the idea mind and the plane of the mind. Thus, the formula for the Law of Unification can be written as follows:

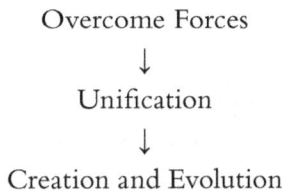

Overcome Forces

↓

Unification

↓

Creation and Evolution

Figure 2.
Law of Unification

Many scientists and physicists have attempted to comprehend the whole existence of the universe by using scientific theories. However, working inside the laboratory of the human form, man can easily gain an understanding of the existence of the universe by following in the footsteps of the creators and by using the Law of Unification. The Law of Unification is the highest law supported by the higher consciousness, and all other laws of creation are formed or created out of this law. The entire universe is governed by a number of laws. Some of these laws are known to man, and some laws are beyond the grasp of the human intelligence. Irrespective of the number of laws governing the creation, the Law of Unification is the sum of all the major laws of the universe. These major laws of creation can be explained with the help of the Law of Unification. It provides for an easy understanding of the process of creation. It does not use mathematical or scientific terms so that it can be understood and applied by every individual to master the process of creation. It combines all the major laws of the universe used for the process of creation.

The Law of Unification is the law of higher consciousness, which controls all the laws of the lower levels of consciousness. Under the influence of the lower levels of consciousness, a man remains a slave to these lower laws. When he works under the directions of the higher consciousness by following the Law of Unification, he is not subjected to the laws operating at the lower levels of consciousness. The Law of

Unification unifies not only the powers of the idea mind and the mind but also all the laws of creation and presents a unique law to be used as a solution to the suffering of man. This unification of all the laws of creation that resulted in a single Law of Unification is presented by the new evolved consciousness to simplify and evolve the life of man. Thus, the Law of Unification can be used by man for his evolution, growth, and fulfillment on this planet.

Unification of the Laws

Because of a lack of understanding of the laws that govern the universe and their improper application, they are often used by man to fulfill the desires originating from the lower levels of consciousness. It is also quite possible for man to misinterpret the meaning and the deeper purpose of the laws. This results in the misapplication of the laws in one's life taking him further away from his growth and evolution. Thus, following the Law of Unification that covers the major laws of creation is a safe path for man to undertake. It can provide him a fulfilling life without any risks of misapplication. The laws that are used for the process of creation are covered under the Law of Unification, and they can be explained with the help of the Law of Unification, as follows:

Law of Divine Oneness

In simple terms, the law of divine oneness explains that everything in the universe is connected and a man creates for himself what he creates for others. By following the Law of Unification, the creators realize the importance of their creations for the benefit of the whole. The understanding of this law itself brings the realization that no being in the universe works only for his own fulfillment, but for the fulfillment of that which encompasses the whole. A single creation created by a single form has the power to raise the consciousness of the whole planet to a higher level, and similarly, a form that is not produced in accordance with the desires of the higher consciousness has the power to bring the consciousness of the whole planet to a lower level. Although man works for his own evolution, he in turn effects the evolution of the whole. The works and creations of the man can never provide him fulfillment if in any way they are not for the benefit of the whole. With the unification of both the minds comes the realization of the working of the whole, which cannot be perceived otherwise.

Law of Inspired Action

The law of inspired action states that in order to create, it is necessary that the action taken by man must be "inspired." "Inspired action" cannot be produced until inspiration is combined with action, which can occur only when the idea mind combines with the mind. This is because inspiration emerge in the plane of the idea mind in the form of new ideas, and these ideas are provided a form in the world of form by the mind. Therefore, the "inspired action" discussed along with the law of inspired action occurs when the ideas of the idea mind produce an inner urge in the creator to give form to the ideas in the world. The urge to take action that is produced by the influence of lower levels of consciousness differs from the "inspired action" that is influenced by the inner urge produced by the ideas of the idea mind. When man follows the Law of Unification for the process of creation, he is not influenced by the lower levels of consciousness. He, thus, works on the new ideas because of the "inspired action" generated within him. This establishes the fact that while following the Law of Unification, the law of inspired action is followed with utmost perfection.

Law of Vibration

According to the law of vibration, if a man can alter his vibrations and match them with the vibrations similar to his desired results, then he can create his desired results in the world of form. The law also guides man to alter his vibrations by changing his thoughts and emotions. Applying the law of vibration in one's life without determining the desires influenced by the lower levels of consciousness is risky, as it does not aid in his evolution. By following the Law of Unification, man works under the guidance of the higher consciousness. The higher consciousness ensures that every individual fulfills his Individual Dharma. The Individual Dharma has a unique vibration that keeps man on the path of his evolution by creating the life and creations necessary for his growth and fulfillment. Further, under the guidance of the higher consciousness, these vibrations result in the creation of evolved and new creations in the world. Following the law of vibration, without fulfilling one's Individual Dharma, results in the fulfillment of the desires of the lower consciousness. Following the Law of Unification ensures that man does not stray away from the path of the higher consciousness, and, thus, constantly works in the higher vibration of the higher consciousness.

Law of Gender

Law of gender states that everything in the universe has masculine and feminine aspects and no creation occurs without the combination of the masculine and the feminine principles. These masculine and feminine aspects involved in the process of creation are observed while understanding the Law of Unification. The masculine aspect is the provider, and the feminine aspect is the receiver. The masculine holds the potential that is manifested through the creative power of the feminine. The plane of the idea mind that provides the new ideas that hold the potential of the new is the masculine aspect in the Law of Unification.

Additionally, the plane of the mind that gives form to the ideas received from the plane of the idea mind to bring the new into existence is the feminine aspect in the Law of Unification. The law of gender guides man to balance the masculine and feminine aspects in order to create forms. But, while following the Law of Unification, the balance of the masculine and feminine aspects is maintained by the higher consciousness for the creators.

Law of Correspondence

The law of correspondence is often stated as "as above so below or as within so without." The use of Law of Unification by the creators demonstrates the flawless working of the law of correspondence. The creators receive the ideas from the higher consciousness that communicates through the plane of the idea mind. Also, they give form to their ideas in the world of form. The ideas that originate from above or at the higher levels of consciousness are given form below or in the world. It illustrates that creation cannot occur if the ideas received from above are not turned into forms below. Similarly, the terms "within" and "without" are used to describe the levels of consciousness. "Above" and "below" explains the levels of consciousness in the context of height. Whereas, "within" and "without" are used to refer to the levels of consciousness in the context of depth. Therefore, above and within refer to higher and deeper levels of consciousness, respectively. Likewise, below and without refer to the lower and shallower levels of consciousness.

❧

Law of Rhythm

The creations move and flow in rhythm. According to the law of rhythm, nothing is constant in the universe. As the seasons change, the external circumstances in a man's life also change. Man should follow the natural rhythm of his life to maintain the flow of creation. The rhythm of creation wavers when the influence of lower levels of consciousness does not let man follow his authentic and natural rhythm. Using the Law of Unification, man can follow his authentic rhythm by fulfilling his Individual Dharma. This makes it easy for him to differentiate between the inauthentic rhythm produced by the influence of the lower levels of consciousness and his natural rhythm. He, thus, cannot be influenced by the lower levels of consciousness and follows the authentic rhythm of higher consciousness joyously. The authentic rhythm generated by the Individual Dharma of man makes him walk on the path of evolution with the least resistance.

❧

Law of Cause and Effect

The law of cause and effect postulates that every cause has an effect and every effect is the result of a cause. But, to comprehend the cause of every experience and the effect of every action, which occurs in a man's life, is out of scope of the limited perception of the human mind. In the functioning of the whole, causes and effects that cannot be understood by the human mind exist. Carl Gustav Jung, discussing the causes and effects that cannot be explained using the law of cause and effect, said, "The philosophical principle that underlies our conception of natural law is causality. But if the connection between cause and effect turns out to be only statistically valid and only relatively true, then the causal principle is only of relative use for explaining natural processes and therefore presupposes the existence of one or more other factors which would be necessary for an explanation. This is as much as to say that the connection of events may in certain circumstances be other than causal, and requires another principle of explanation."[11]

This statement by Carl Gustav Jung does not nullify the law of cause and effect but elucidates that there are scenarios when the cause or effect cannot be determined with the help of the law of cause and effect. These causes and effects that cannot be deciphered by the human mind also play a significant role in the functioning of the whole. Moreover, consciousness ensures that even if man is unable to keep an account of the causes and effects that may help him in his evolution, his Individual Dharma guides him toward his evolution. The higher consciousness functions for the evolution of the whole and maintains the account of causes and effects necessary for this evolution. Using the Law of Unification, man works under the guidance of higher consciousness and fulfills his Individual Dharma that stores the causes and effects necessary for his evolution and the evolution of the whole. When man uses the law of cause and effect to fulfill the desires of lower consciousness, he hinders the functioning and evolution of the whole. When following the Law of Unification, the higher consciousness ensures that man walks on the path of evolution while following all the laws of creation effortlessly.

> "It is better to strive in one's own dharma than to succeed in another's dharma. Nothing is ever lost in following one's own dharma."[12]
>
> The Bhagavad Gita

Chapter - 4
Planes and Forces

Planes of Idea Mind and Mind

When the evolutionary process created the human form, the human form was provided with a unit called "mind." Due to its continuous involvement in man's life, the human mind has become quite reliable to each individual for seeking solutions to his questions and problems. Because of this reason, man's reliance on his mind has grown immensely. But, the solution to his every problem cannot be found while working within the limits of the human mind. Likewise, every question that arises in the mind cannot be answered with the help of the limited reasoning of the human mind. Therefore, the creators never depend solely on the human mind for the purpose of creation. The creators have awareness of the plane that provides new perception to the problems of the world in a new space and new ideas, which can be used for new creations in the world. This another plane can be conceived as another mind that is not bounded by the concepts and limits of the human mind.

Sir Arthur Stanley Eddington, the famous physicist and astronomer, stated that "The universe is of the nature of 'a thought or sensation in a universal Mind'."[13] In the preceding statement, the "universal mind" that Sir Arthur Stanley Eddington referred to is the plane of the idea mind and the "thought or sensation" is the idea appearing in that plane. Further elaborating on the statement given by Sir Arthur Stanley Eddington, it can be said that the universe is a creation, that first appeared as a thought or sensation in a universal mind. Also, as all creations first appear as ideas in the plane of the idea mind before they are provided a form, the statement is pointing toward the process of creation.

Everything is first created in the idea mind. The idea mind is the mind through which the higher consciousness tries to connect with the human mind so that the creations that exist in the idea mind as ideas can be transformed into forms or frameworks using the powers of the mind. Therefore, ideas play a key role in the process of creation. The idea is a connection established by the higher consciousness with the ones who are open and receptive to receive the new. Ideas originate in the plane of the idea mind represented by wings in the forms of Creator Gods and Deities of ancient mythology, which is discussed in Chapter 2 of the book. It is the expanse and space which the creators and geniuses explore to find ideas for their new creations.

Man spends most of his life living in the plane of the mind—thinking, judging, calculating, analyzing, and so on. When the unit, that is, "the mind" was provided to the man, it was meant to be used as a tool. But, as man started relying on the mind for every small decision, the role gets reversed and the mind now attempts to make man his tool. Mind has innumerable powers that can be used according to the role man assigns to it but if the mind starts assigning the work to the man, the evolution of the man will be hindered. Man's work is to fulfill his Individual Dharma for his evolution and growth. The Individual Dharma dictates the work to be accomplished by an individual so that he can become a creator and use the powers of his mind. The human mind tries to judge all aspects of experiences it encounters. Therefore, when it is presented with the new ideas from the plane of the idea mind to fulfill his Individual Dharma, it often rejects them if they do not fit in the domain of its limited and rigid reasoning. When the mind does not find enough reason to justify the importance of the new, it dismisses it. This acts as an obstruction on the path of evolution of the man and the whole.

Therefore, in order to aid the process of evolution and create the new, the mind must be ready to receive the new. The powers of the mind are required to be used in cooperation with the powers of the idea mind to create. The powers of the mind when used alone are insufficient to accomplish the process of creation. The plane of the mind, which is material in nature, is used for the purpose of materialization of the creative ideas received from the plane of the idea mind. The unification of the powers of both the planes makes creation possible. The resistance of the mind toward the new is the result of the effect of forces acting upon it from the lower levels of consciousness. Man lives under the influence of these forces and unknowingly works under their effects. The mind and the idea mind cannot work together and unify their powers until man overcomes the hindrances in the form of forces of the lower levels of consciousness. Hence, it is essential for man to overcome the forces inhibiting unification so that he can work under the guidance of the higher consciousness that interacts through the plane of the idea mind to create new creations.

Forces of Lower Consciousness

Once the man chooses the path of mastering creation using the Law of Unification, he should acquaint himself with the forces that act upon him from the lower levels of consciousness and obstruct the unification of the minds. Because of the effect of the forces acting upon them, the human mind and the old frameworks acquire stubbornness and become resistant toward receiving the new. The anxiety, stress, and mental problems man suffers from in today's world is the result of this unnecessary clinging to the frameworks and models that are obsolete and no longer serve the planet and its evolution. The more the stubbornness of the human mind or the frameworks, the more fiercely consciousness has to break through them so as to create the new. During the process of evolution, the old frameworks may shatter if consciousness has to move forcefully through forms because of their resistance. Therefore, to save the frameworks from forcefully getting shattered and to make the process of evolution a smooth transition of established frameworks into new forms, it is necessary to overcome the forces of the lower levels of consciousness. The forces are discussed below in detail.

Beliefs

While walking on the path of evolution and creation, man needs to re-examine the beliefs that are formed on the basis of activities performed by the external environment or the thoughts originating from the lower levels of consciousness. When man blindly puts his beliefs into practice, he becomes a slave to those beliefs. The beliefs not inquired are the forces that act on an individual to prevent him from taking a higher step on the ladder of consciousness. They are the hidden chains that bind man to the lower levels of consciousness and hinder his growth and evolution. For beliefs, if strongly held, can become an unrealistic support structure for man, which will plummet as soon as the beliefs are proved wrong.

Beliefs are majorly developed during the growing years of an individual. These beliefs guide the opinions he constructs in his life. The firmly held opinions do not let man use the powers of the idea mind. He, thus, feels trapped in the limited domains of the mind. A person with a strongly held belief system, formed without adequate inquiry, cannot work upon new ideas to create new forms and frameworks. This is because the new is born through the space that is experienced when the mind is not trapped in the limits of the beliefs. Beliefs are the ideas stored in the mind operating around the lower levels of consciousness, unlike the ideas provided by the higher consciousness originating in the plane of the idea mind. When the mind is clouded with beliefs, it is unable to see the new ideas approaching from the plane of the idea mind. To make progress on the path of creation and evolution, it is necessary to leave the beliefs that no longer serve one's evolution.

While walking on the path of mastering creation, creators must not cling to the old beliefs and focus all their attention upon the new that is approaching from the plane of the idea mind. The old beliefs can block the flow of new ideas that hold the power to bring fulfillment to man. The new ideas are rejected because of man's fear due to his uninquired beliefs. When the force of belief is powerful enough to convince the mind that the new that does not fit with the beliefs of man can bring loss, failure, or criticism, then the mind rejects the new because of fear. The fear is the by-product of the forces of lower levels of consciousness. Thus, when the beliefs that do not serve the evolution and creation are discarded, the fear in the mind automatically ceases to exist. It is, therefore, necessary to inquire before a belief is formed.

Desires

Similar to beliefs, desires that originate from the lower levels of consciousness obstruct the unification of the minds. When man is influenced by the force of desires originating from the lower levels of consciousness, he starts to consider the fulfillment of these desires as the only purpose of his life. Alternatively, the creators work to fulfill the desires of the higher consciousness by following the Law of Unification. This, as a result, fulfills the highest desire of evolution and creation. But it cannot be accomplished when the man's attention is pulled by the force of desires of lower consciousness, and he keeps working for the fulfillment of these desires.

The only desires that can bring fulfillment and growth are the desires of the higher consciousness. The desires that originate from the lower levels of consciousness are substitute desires. These desires are perceived by man as a way of attaining fulfillment. But, even when man attains these desires, they do not bring fulfillment. Thus, the desires of the higher consciousness, through which fulfillment and satisfaction are achieved, are crushed beneath the weight of the substitute desires of the lower levels of consciousness.

On the path of evolution, creators only work for the fulfillment of the desires of the higher consciousness. The desires approaching from the higher levels of consciousness bring peace and calm along with them. Also, such desires are fulfilled effortlessly. This is a simple way to identify whether the desires are approaching from higher levels of consciousness or whether they are the substitute desires coming from lower levels of consciousness. When the creators work under the guidance of higher consciousness and accomplish the higher desires, they attain fulfillment in their lives. While working for the fulfillment of the higher desires, the desires of the lower levels of consciousness lose their influence and effect on the creators. Therefore, the creators are only concerned with the fulfillment of their "Individual Dharma" and the creation of the new.

The substitute desires originating from the lower levels of consciousness are fulfilled by possessing the object or goal that is desired. The desires of higher levels of consciousness are fulfilled by providing, creating, and evolving. Moreover, freedom is associated with the fulfillment of the desires of higher levels of consciousness. On the other hand, when the desires produced because of the lower levels of consciousness are fulfilled by man, they turn him into his slave.

Attachments

The biggest threat to the evolution of man is his attachment to the old forms and frameworks, which does not let him move toward the higher levels of consciousness and establish these higher levels in the world of form by creating new creations. Attachments are the chains that bind man in disguise of providing him comfort and security. Often, man mistakes attachments for love. This confusion of considering attachments as love is presented by the lower levels of consciousness to keep man under its influence. However, with the help of clear perception originating from the plane of the idea mind, man can easily outgrow the old. He is, thus, able to discard the attachments to old forms and frameworks that do not serve his evolution.

There are three major reasons for man's inability to discard the attachments that act as a hindrance on the path of his evolution. These reasons are discussed in the following sections.

1). Dependency

Man's resolute attachments to the old patterns and frameworks is because of his dependency on people, things, environment, or forms. These dependencies remain with man throughout his life not because they cannot be removed but because the removal of the old is not considered an important element in one's growth and the old feels familiar and comfortable to him. For the arrival and establishment of the "New," the old patterns, frameworks, and structures need to be discarded. As the world becomes more and more independent, man should learn to enjoy freedom and independence. The new creations can be brought into existence when the dependency is neither on the external environment nor on the inner thoughts that arise because of the influence of lower levels of consciousness.

2). Habits

The repetitive patterns of man's actions or responses are stored in the lower levels of consciousness that influence the actions taken by man in his life. The patterns originating from the lower levels of consciousness control the decisions and actions of man. Man's body and mind are the storehouse of the actions and responses generated by him over a period of time. These actions and responses are known as habits. As man becomes used to doing a task in a certain way, or living his life in a certain manner, it becomes difficult for him to leave these old habits even when they are obstructing his evolution. Because of these habits, man rejects the new ideas that approach from the plane of the idea mind. These habits provide a sense of comfort to man because of which he is unable to get rid of his old attachments.

3). Security

Security is one of the basic needs of man, and change is perceived as the biggest threat to his security. But the change that guides man to reach a higher state of existence must not be feared. One must move as the consciousness desires him to move for the evolution of self and the whole. This can happen only if he discards the old notions of security and embraces evolving consciousness that knows the way to reach the state of higher existence. Everything that is created in the world of form is mortal; therefore, security cannot be found in the forms or frameworks. To seek security in the forms that are not constant can only lead man to a state of dissatisfaction. Therefore, the only thing good enough to seek is "evolution" in the world of form, where nothing is permanent and everything is changing and evolving.

Walking on the path of mastering creation requires the use of the idea mind as well as the mind. Certain qualities of the mind should be watched out for while using the Law of Unification. One of these qualities is the fickleness of mind. The mind may try to distract man from his path toward evolution because of its variable nature. But if one is earnest in his attempt to reach his goal, no forces can stop him from accomplishing unification and becoming a creator of the new.

> "And be not conformed to this world: but be ye transformed by the renewing of your mind, that ye may prove what is that good, and acceptable, and perfect, will of God."[14]
>
> King James Version

Chapter - 5
Powers of the Idea Mind and the Mind

Powers of the Idea Mind

Power of Wisdom

*W*isdom is intuitive intelligence, which is not based on reasoning of human mind. It is knowledge supported by higher consciousness and does not fit in the domains of human mind. Man has always been blessed with the power of wisdom, but he seldom uses it as he remains unaware of its presence throughout his life. The law of higher consciousness that is followed by the creators cannot be used by man without the power of wisdom of the idea mind. The power of wisdom of the idea mind expands the perceptions of man beyond the limits of logical reasoning and rational thinking of the mind. The power of wisdom is the higher knowledge of the higher consciousness required for taking important decisions in life to walk on the path of evolution and creation. Wisdom is the ability to differentiate between the desires of the higher consciousness and the desires that originate from lower levels of consciousness. Without the power of wisdom, the creators cannot walk on the path of evolution and creation without getting influenced by the forces of lower levels of consciousness.

Man recognizes his function and contribution in the working of the whole through the power of wisdom. This recognition is a source of fulfillment and satisfaction when performing the works of higher consciousness. Man's Individual Dharma presents him with circumstances and experiences in life that aid in providing various revelations. These revelations are presented to man in the form of wisdom. Wisdom cannot be developed, as it is omnipresent in man. It is revealed to man only when he is able to comprehend the lessons designed exclusively for his evolution by following his Individual Dharma.

A man possessing extensive knowledge is not in touch with the power of wisdom of the idea mind if he is unaware of the most efficient way of using that knowledge for his growth and evolution. Such a man works under the influence of lower levels of consciousness and uses his knowledge to fulfill the desires of lower levels of consciousness. The knowledge acquired through the mind needs the support and guidance of the wisdom present in the plane of the idea mind for creation of the new and evolution of man. Wisdom keeps one on the path of his evolution and growth by utilizing the knowledge of the mind beneficially. The suffering is caused when man solely depends upon the knowledge of the mind for taking decisions in his life. By using the power of wisdom, man can easily find his way out of suffering. Wisdom is boundless, and even when it appears irrational to the mind, it is able to take man out of his self-created suffering. On the other hand, even though when knowledge appears rational, it motivates him to take the most foolish decisions of life and puts him on the path of even greater chaos and suffering. The wisdom originating from the idea mind reaches all those who are open to receive and use it while following "Individual Dharma." As the guidance provided by the wisdom often contradicts the knowledge of the mind, it is, therefore, necessary to unify the powers of knowledge and of wisdom to create the new.

Power of Provision

Provision is an idea stored in the plane of the idea mind, which has the potential to be manifested in the world of form. Provisions can be used to create new forms, frameworks, and models. Provisions are not mere imaginary forms or images, they are the reflection of the world yet to be manifested and created by the creators. Provisions are provided to man through different ways. These ideas are received in dreams, visions, or through subtle knowledge and understanding. Those who possess the courage to use the power of provision and transform the ideas into new creations using the Law of Unification are the creators, the inventors, and the masters of creation. When the provision is received by the mind and worked upon using the powers of the mind, new creations are brought to the world. The provision brings along a strong sense of purpose for the creators, which increases levels of efficiency and perseverance in creators while they work for the evolution of the whole.

Everything required by man to live a fulfilled life is stored in the plane of the idea mind as provisions and can be used to attain fulfillment and satisfaction. The provisions contain the solution for man's suffering, responses that are not influenced by lower levels of consciousness, and the decisions that aid man on the path of his evolution and growth. The idea mind continuously provides man with new ideas, which he is unable to use because of the forces of lower levels of consciousness that keep him bound to lower planes. The forces keep the understanding of man buried under their influence and limit his perception. Thus, man is unable to receive the provisions offered by the plane of the idea mind. To facilitate the process of evolution and guide man on the path of creation, the ideas provided by the idea mind reach man in ways that appear mysterious to the mind. The provisions of the idea mind do not reach man in loud or rational ways, and therefore, they are often missed among the noise of thoughts originating from lower levels of consciousness. The power of provision can be easily accessed through the plane of the idea mind. Consciousness takes care of the needs of all and also provides man with new ideas or provisions for his growth, evolution, and fulfillment.

The idea mind is the provider and the guide for man. It contains solutions to man's problems and facilitates his growth. Man takes his decisions based upon either the ideas stored in the subconscious mind or the rational and logical reasoning of the mind. As a result, his decisions and choices do not reflect his Individual Dharma that obstructs his evolution. When decisions and choices of man are based upon provisions of the idea mind, instead of submitting to the reasoning of the mind or conditioning of the subconscious mind, he is then able to walk the path of evolution effortlessly and create new creations for the world, and thus, fulfill his Individual Dharma.

Powers of the Mind

Power of Knowledge

The human mind is a huge reservoir of information acquired through various means from the external world. The information stored in the human mind cannot guide man regarding the decisions he needs to take in his life that can aid in his evolution, but it can be used to produce forms and frameworks in the world. This information acquired from external sources, stored in the plane of the mind, is the power of knowledge of the mind and is used by the creators to give form to the ideas in the world. The power of knowledge of the mind is as important in the process of creation as the power of wisdom of the idea mind.

The power of knowledge is the knowledge of the world of form. It is developed when a human mind learns from direct or indirect experiences through different channels. This power of knowledge when used in collaboration with the power of wisdom of the idea mind results in the creation of an evolved life, and further, it brings new creations into existence for the evolution of the whole. The power of knowledge of the mind provides information about the activities that take place in the world and the functioning of the world of form. This knowledge includes the information regarding the working of societies, different structures and cultures, different areas of study, and everything that is found in the world of form necessary to be learned for living in the world. Therefore, by gaining the knowledge of the world, man is able to learn the ways and language of the world that can be used by him to bring new creations to the world of form in a language or way easily understandable by his fellow men. The power of knowledge when developed by man can be used to give form to the ideas that can then be turned into creations for the world.

But, even with all the knowledge gained from the world, man cannot become a creator of the new life and new creations if the power of knowledge of the mind is not backed by the power of wisdom of the idea mind. When the power of knowledge of the mind is not monitored by the power of wisdom of the idea mind, it can result in the ill-use of power of knowledge in the world of form. It may further cause more suffering and destruction in the world instead of supporting the process of creation. While the world operates under the influence of the lower levels of consciousness, it is necessary to use the knowledge gained through the world in cooperation with the power of wisdom that approaches from higher levels of consciousness. Therefore, the power of knowledge needs to be utilized together with the power of wisdom for the evolution of the whole.

Power of Expression

The process of evolution through the creation of new forms, frameworks, or models can be accomplished when the desires of the higher consciousness are expressed by man through the creation of the new. The new creations brought into the world must be able to express the higher ways of the higher consciousness. In order to make this possible, the power of expression of the mind is used to give form to the ideas approaching from the plane of the idea mind. The provisions from the plane of the idea mind require the power of expression of the mind so that they can be expressed in this world. Creators use the power of expression to express the ideas received from the plane of the idea mind by using language, art, or any other form of expression. By using the power of expression, creators also express their Individual Dharma. As every individual has different characteristics and traits, each individual's Individual Dharma is a unique expression of those characteristics and traits.

The power of expression can be developed by training the mind in various subjects and pursuits. The perception of both the external world and the idea plays a significant role in the way a creator expresses the ideas received from the plane of the idea mind. Thus, each idea is expressed uniquely by each individual. The limitations of the mind can be surpassed by using the power of expression of the mind in cooperation with the power of provision to express unique and new ideas provided by the higher levels of consciousness. The more the individual maintains the originality of idea through his expression, the more the limitations decrease.

The truest expression of the higher levels of consciousness can be created in the world of form when the power of provision of the plane of idea mind works with the power of expression of the plane of mind. A creator does not only create new forms that are an expression of the higher levels of consciousness but also his life that is an expression of his highest self. The creations created thus are a source of fulfillment for the creator and the world.

Idea Mind and Subconscious Mind

Whenever powers of the mind are discussed, the subconscious plane of mind and its powers are often considered an important part of the discussion. As the powers of both the planes of the idea mind and the mind are discussed in this chapter, a discussion to differentiate the functions and uses of the plane of the idea mind from that of the plane of the subconscious mind is also required, so that the plane of idea mind is not confused with the plane of subconscious mind.

The use of subconscious mind for changing or altering the conditionings in man has already been discussed in Chapter 1 of the book. The subconscious mind is powerful enough to achieve its designated tasks, but it is not conscious enough to decide the path that can lead him toward his evolution. Even the conscious mind that is at a higher level than the subconscious plane of mind is only a tool for man that can aid in the evolution, but it cannot provide man the ideas that will lead to evolution and growth. The plane of the idea mind, on the other hand, is the provider and the guide that knows the path leading toward the evolution of the whole.

The subconscious mind is similar to a powerful mechanical operator that will follow the instructions provided to it, irrespective of whether they lead to growth or destruction. Therefore, man uses his subconscious mind for achieving success or attaining the desired goals by providing instructions to it. But the desires of man, which urge him to instruct the subconscious mind to work toward the attainment of goals, originate from lower levels of consciousness. The desires originating from the higher levels of consciousness come from the plane of idea mind that can be accessed by following the Law of Unification.

The idea mind does not follow instructions as the subconscious mind, rather it provides directions to man so that he can walk on the path of evolution. When the subconscious mind operates according to the instructions provided to it from lower levels of consciousness, it obstructs the evolution of man. It not only obstructs, but in certain cases, can work against the movements of consciousness to fulfill the demands of lower levels of consciousness. Hence, the use of subconscious mind is not recommended until or unless the instructions that are provided to it come from the higher levels of consciousness.

The plane of the idea mind guides man through the power of wisdom and the power of provision. The idea mind is the inner Guru who guides every individual on the path of his evolution by providing him directions to fulfill his Individual Dharma and become a creator.

When man follows the directions and guidance of the inner Guru and works for the evolution of the whole, new creations are brought to the world. Moreover, it occurs when the plane of mind unifies with the plane of idea mind. For the unification of both the planes of mind, the powers of the plane of mind must overcome the forces of lower levels of consciousness so that they can work in cooperation with the powers of the plane of idea mind, as stated by the Law of Unification.

Part II

Practicing Unification

"Freedom to pass back and forth across the world division, from the perspective of the apparitions of time to that of the causal deep and back—not contaminating the principles of the one with those of the other, yet permitting the mind to know the one by virtue of the other—is the talent of the master."[15]

Joseph Campbell

Chapter - 6
Overcoming Forces

Willpower

Man fritters away his energy and time when he tries to fight with the forces of the lower levels of consciousness. Therefore, instead of fighting these forces, it is best to overcome them. This can be accomplished with the help of willpower. Willpower exists in every human form, but only a few utilize it wisely. It is a seed that is planted in all human forms to overcome the influences of the lower levels of consciousness, but it must be watered to reap its benefits. The development of potentialities present in man largely depends on the magnitude of his willpower. There are innumerable potentialities hidden within man, waiting to be explored and utilized for the evolution. Rarely is man aware that the key to grow and use these potentialities lies within the grasp of his own willpower.

The willpowers existing in the two planes—the plane of idea mind and the plane of mind—are different and have separate uses in the process of creation and evolution. The willpower of the mind has been provided to man to rise above the forces of the lower levels of consciousness. Due to the influence of these forces, man is often manipulated to use the willpower of the plane of the mind to fulfill the desires produced by lower levels of consciousness. This takes him further away from his evolution and results in producing suffering and distortion in his life. Therefore, the willpower of the mind must be used to overcome the forces of lower levels of consciousness before the unification of minds can occur. On the other hand, the willpower present in the plane of the idea mind cannot be used until the unification of minds has occurred. Once the minds are unified, the willpower of the plane of idea mind takes control of the willpower of the plane of mind. Thus, the willpower of the idea mind is used to accomplish the process of creation for the fulfillment of desires of higher consciousness.

Various forces that originate from the lower levels of consciousness influence man. These forces have a tendency to draw the consciousness of the man toward themselves. This confuses him, as he is unable to distinguish between the works influenced by the higher consciousness and those by the forces of the lower levels of consciousness. The engulfing forces are so strong that often man loses himself in them and spends his life under their influence, thus fulfilling the desires of lower levels of consciousness. However, even if man fights these forces using his willpower, they only tend to grow in power and, therefore, make him helpless. Man's willpower should not be used to fight or resist the forces of lower levels of consciousness but to draw his consciousness toward the plane of idea mind and overcome the influence of these forces. It then establishes a connection with the higher levels of consciousness. Before using the willpower of mind to rise above the forces of lower levels of consciousness, it must be excercised. Exercising the willpower requires conscious effort, and it can be done through some simple yet effective ways, as follows.

❦

Exercising Willpower

Meet Commitments

According to the Hindu mythology, an era known as "Sat (Truth) Yuga (Age)" existed on the planet. During this era, men used to have a deep commitment to their word. They did what they promised and were always true to their word. It is also said that the needs of the people living in this era were fulfilled by the word they spoke. This manifestation did not happen magically. Their willpower helped them to fulfill their commitments, and ultimately, it became a law to be followed by the whole age.

Willpower can be improved by avoiding the tendency of making commitments, to oneself or other people, that one is unable to fulfill. Not committing to anything that one is unsure of fulfilling is a way to practice self-control. Although man is always taught to follow his commitments to avoid any inconveniences, the essence of this teaching lies in the fact that fulfilling commitments is an ancient technique of exercising willpower.

Reduce Complexity

As life becomes more complicated, the distractions that draw the consciousness of man toward themselves also increase. Many times, man remains unaware of the thoughts, forms, or objects that pull his consciousness toward them, and he finds himself entangled in them. To exercise willpower, a clear mind is necessary. Even when his external environment is complex, the complexity of mind can be reduced by not focusing on the thoughts that are not needed at the moment and attributing attention to a single task at hand.

Willpower can also be used to handle complex relationships in life. Every person one meets in life or establishes a relationship with is meant to aid in his evolution and growth. Once the relationship fulfills its purpose, it fades away. If man tries to cling on to such a relationship, he invites complexity into his life and obstructs his evolution. Any life circumstance or situation that needs to be dispersed but is held due to the forces of lower levels of consciousness increases the complexity in a man's life.

Letting go of the old and focusing one's attention on the current tasks or relationships reduces the complexity in life, and thus, enables man to exercise his willpower.

Limit Futile Talks

There are various forms of "futile talks" that do not result in the evolution of life. Rather, they drag the energy out of one's self and become a self-deteriorating practice. Fault-finding is a form of futile talk that not only ruins the mental health of the doer but also destroys his relationships within which it is performed. The effort and energy used by man to find faults in others can be effectively utilized in doing some constructive work.

Gossiping is yet another example of futile talks that does not yield any valuable results in the life of man. Wasting one's energy in gossiping leads to various mental health issues. As the contemporary culture is fueled with discussions and sharing of information, futile talks have become an unconscious practice. Keeping a check on one's tendency to get involved in unnecessary talks is a great exercise for the development of willpower. Man can exercise his willpower by being aware of the time and energy he spends in the talks that deteriorate his mind and his nervous system, and thus, keeping himself from getting involved in these talks.

Check Overindulgence

The senses are provided to man to enjoy the world of form. But when this satisfaction of the senses becomes the sole purpose of his existence, he becomes a victim of overindulgence. Enjoying life is a necessary part of living a fulfilled life, but one should not get attached to the pleasures of the world. Today, man is surrounded not only by the world of form that appears to provide satisfaction through pleasures but also by another virtual world that appears to provide him satisfaction through virtual pleasures. Although social media is useful to access information and connect with the world, its unrestricted usage can result in an unconscious overindulgence in the virtual pleasures that appear to be a source of fulfillment.

Virtual world is a world where man can virtually talk, share information, or connect with other people. The more he indulges himself in the virtual connections of the virtual world, the more he experiences a lack of authentic connection in his life—the connection with the plane of the idea mind. Due to overindulgence in these pleasures, man is unable to establish a connection with the idea mind. Man can exercise his willpower rigorously if he keeps a check on his overindulgences, and this will support him in establishing a connection with the plane of the idea mind.

Regulate Daydreaming

Daydreaming occurs when the thoughts originating from the lower levels of consciousness pull a man's attention and takes him into an imaginary world of past or future. There is a difference between daydreaming and wondering about an idea originating from the idea mind to find an expression to give it a form in the world. Daydreaming pulls a man's attention into a virtual world, which causes his awareness to decline. On the other hand, finding an expression for the idea is a conscious practice carried out by creators to find solutions to the problems of the world. Often, daydreaming becomes a habit as man starts to enjoy the imaginary life of the dreamworld and disconnects from the real world. When man squanders his time in daydreaming, he becomes less conscious, and as a result starts to work around lower levels of consciousness. By being conscious of his daydreaming tendencies and by not letting his attention to be pulled by the thoughts originating from lower levels of consciousness, man can exercise and develop his willpower.

By exercising the willpower using the aforementioned methods, man is able to

1) discriminate between the desires of lower levels of consciousness and of the higher consciousness, 2) attain a dispassionate temperament toward the forces of lower levels of consciousness, and 3) achieve a heightened level of awareness. These three qualities,

namely the qualities of discrimination, dispassion, and heightened awareness, help man rise above the forces of lower levels of consciousness that act as a major hindrance in the unification of the idea mind and the mind.

∞

Rising Above the Forces

Discrimination

While exercising willpower using the aforementioned practices, man may observe subtle changes in his perception. These changes help in building an acute sense of discrimination in man, which is necessary to identify the forces of lower levels of consciousness. These forces cannot be overcome until they are not identified. Even when man has the theoretical knowledge of the forces originating from lower levels of consciousness, he will not be able to identify them within himself or around himself if he has not developed the sense of discrimination through the practices. The subtle changes found in the perception because of exercising willpower also help man in distinguishing the movements of higher consciousness from that of the lower levels of consciousness. This discrimination makes it easier for him to work according to the higher consciousness while accomplishing the task of creation and evolution. This discrimination enables man to rise above the forces that keep him bound to the lower levels of consciousness and to discard the old. Thus, he can connect with the plane of idea mind and create the new using the new ideas.

⚬⚬⚬

Dispassion

Dispassion, in context of rising above the forces, does not mean suppressing any passion that man has in life for enjoyment. But it means becoming dispassionate toward the forces of lower levels of consciousness so that they are unable to influence man on his path of evolution. When man exercises the willpower and develops the quality of discrimination, he is able to attain some amount of self-control, which, in turn, helps him in becoming dispassionate toward the forces originating from lower levels of consciousness. Therefore, their impact upon him also decreases. The quality of dispassion is also necessary while working on the problems to create new solutions. This is because passion creates entanglements with the object or situation one is working on passionately. Hence, creators must work dispassionately while creating a new solution for their problems, otherwise they may find themselves entangled in the problems they are working upon. For the evolution of the whole, creators remain dispassionate toward the forces and problems originating from the lower levels of consciousness and create new solutions under the guidance of higher consciousness by bringing ideas from the plane of idea mind.

⚬⚬⚬

Heightened Awareness

The body and mind of man, over time, get used to the responses and reactions of their human form and, therefore, work unconsciously. When man starts exercising his willpower, he becomes more aware of the responses and reactions that his human form produces. However, too much control of senses in exercising willpower can result in the suppression of the senses, which is beneficial neither for the senses of man nor for the human form. But exercising willpower using the practices discussed in the previous section enables man to maintain the amount of control necessary to reach a heightened level of awareness. When man works from a heightened level of awareness, the forces of lower levels of consciousness cannot influence him. Heightened awareness helps man to rise above these forces. Also, when the level of awareness in a man increases, he is able understand the causes of suffering and distortion. He is able to see clearly the influences approaching from the lower levels of consciousness. This helps him in overcoming the forces. Thus, heightened awareness is a major quality that can be utilized to overcome the forces and accomplish the unification of minds to master the process of creation.

Chapter - 7
Accelerating Unification

For the unification of minds, man has to establish a connection with the plane of the idea mind through which the higher consciousness provides new ideas for creation and evolution. Once the connection is established with the plane of idea mind, the new ideas provided by the idea mind are needed to be brought into existence using the powers of mind. To accomplish this, the following procedure must be pursued persistently with patience and humility.

❧

Preparing to Connect with Idea Mind

Restfulness

Man was created from restfulness, and he enters the state again when his human form stops functioning; if he learns to act through restfulness, he will understand the highest law of creation. Restfulness does not refer to non-activity nor does it mean despising every action in the world, but it refers to that space which is the origin of every action. Restfulness exists behind every action. As man today is living in a competitive framework designed by the civilization, he keeps wanting to acquire more. The lack of restfulness results in diminishing creative tendencies in man. This is because restlessness does not allow man to connect with the idea mind and receive new ideas for creating the new.

Thus, the life whose foundation is laid on running around and competing can only be sustained if one continuously does so. This continuous running and competing is also a cause of increasing levels of anxiety observed in man today. When competition is the foundation of life, it is impossible for man to rest. Therefore, if man wants to turn his life into a creation instead of a competition, he must create his life based on the ideas received by entering the state of restfulness. The life that is created according to the ideas originating from restfulness keeps man in the state of restfulness even while he is working or acting in the world.

Today, man has a beautiful gift of being able to communicate his thoughts and share it with the world through various channels. But, too much information hinders the unification of minds. This is because excessive amounts of information result in restlessness. It prevents him from entering the state of restfulness where he can receive new ideas for the creation of the new. To clearly perceive the ideas that approach man from the plane of the idea mind for his evolution, the disturbances in the human form must be removed by restfulness, which is required by man so that he can directly listen to the guidance of the higher consciousness and follow his Individual Dharma without being influenced by lower levels of consciousness. The state of restfulness cannot be achieved using willpower, as restfulness is experienced through yielding. The willpower, thus, is exercised to rise above the forces of lower levels of consciousness by developing the qualities of discrimination, dispassion, and heightened awareness, and not for connecting with the idea mind.

Solitude

Another state that is necessary to receive the ideas from the plane of the idea mind is solitude. Solitude is the quality of being comfortable in spending time with oneself. Spending time alone with one's own self is something that most people dread. They are fearful of the thoughts or emotions that may originate when they spend time in solitude. But to connect with the plane of the idea mind, man must learn to spend some time in solitude. The ideas from the plane of the idea mind do not approach man while he is partying or enjoying the pleasures of the world. The new ideas that approach from higher consciousness come from the plane of idea mind that can be accessed through solitude. The famous scientist and genius Albert Einstein understood the importance of solitude in the process of creation, as he said, "I lived in solitude ... and noticed how the monotony of a quiet life stimulates the creative mind."[16] The ideas that approach man from the limited domains of mind are fueled by lower levels of consciousness. Solitude decreases the influence of thoughts and information generated by lower levels of consciousness coming from the external world.

This does not mean that man should not collaborate and work alone. But if man wants to create, he must not force himself to work in collaboration until he has established a connection with the idea mind that provides him with new ideas. When he has established connection with the idea mind, the new ideas can be given form either with the help of collaborations or alone, as per the requirement of the work of creation. In case man has not connected with the plane of the idea mind, the work he does is influenced by lower levels of consciousness and does not result in the creation of new models and frameworks. Similarly, the collaborations formed without first establishing a connection with the idea mind are used to perform the work of lower levels of consciousness. Solitude makes it easier for man to identify the thoughts that do not serve the evolution and discard them while connecting with the idea mind. Therefore, to devote oneself to spend time in solitude is an important part of the process of creation, as new ideas cannot be forced out of the idea mind when man is influenced by the external world.

Connecting with Idea Mind

While man prepares to connect with the plane of idea mind using restfulness and solitude, streams of thoughts that try to keep him bound to the old start appearing in his consciousness. Man has to move past these thoughts to connect with the plane of the idea mind. The following steps are required to be followed to reach the plane of idea mind.

Step 1: Reflection

Many times, man gets engaged and involved in the tasks of the world by following the majority and considering these acts as the sole aim of his life. Although he may receive the knowledge of the world by observing and learning from the majority, he can connect with the wisdom of the idea mind and gain the understanding of his path toward evolution only by engaging in a thorough reflection of his thoughts and actions in the world. If man experiences a lack of fulfillment, then it is a result of resistance toward his evolution. It also signifies that man is not creating according to the desires of the higher consciousness. For becoming a creator of the new, the practice of reflection is of utmost importance. The questions to reflect on are as follows:

1) Am I creating my life around lower levels of consciousness?
2) Which thoughts or opinions stop me from creating the new according to the higher consciousness?
3) Are these thoughts or opinions influenced by the forces of the lower levels of consciousness?

After reflecting, he will be able to determine whether he is creating his life as per his Individual Dharma and also whether the knowledge that he uses is supported by the power of wisdom of the idea mind. Using reflection and the sense of discrimination, man can easily identify the thoughts, opinions, or actions that obstruct the creation and evolution.

Step 2: Ignoring Unserviceable Thoughts

If man becomes aware that he is not able to create the new because of the influence of certain thoughts, opinions, or actions that do not support his evolution, then he needs to discard these old and unserviceable thoughts. It means that he must now ignore the thoughts or opinions that act as an obstruction on the path of his evolution. By living in the society, man acquires a number of conditionings that produce a regular stream of thoughts that act as an obstruction in the creation of the new. Disregarding the thoughts that do not serve the purpose of creation helps man in reaching the plane of idea mind. The states of restfulness and solitude can be used to observe the stream of thoughts before ignoring the ones that obstruct evolution. Restfulness and solitude reduce the influence of unserviceable thoughts. Thus, the connection with the plane of the idea mind is established through which the higher consciousness provides the new ideas for the fulfillment of one's Individual Dharma and for the evolution of the whole.

Step 3: Emergence of New Ideas

After moving past the old and unserviceable thoughts, man reaches the plane of the idea mind. This plane of the idea mind provides new ideas through dreams, visions, or subtle understanding that can be used to make choices and take decisions in one's life that help to fulfill one's Individual Dharma and become the creator of new life and new creations. When man has something so vast and free to depend upon for the provisions of his life, he himself starts to live a worriless and free existence. But, even after he has completed the task of connecting himself with the plane of the idea mind, the human mind may interfere in the work of giving form to the ideas when it rejects the new ideas that do not fit within the limits of its reasoning and logic. Therefore, to prevent the rejection of the new ideas approaching from the plane of the idea mind, the plane of the mind must be prepared for receiving the ideas. In order to receive the new ideas coming from the idea mind and give them form in the world, the following qualities are necessary:

Receiving Ideas and Creating

Openness

Although new ideas are provided by the idea mind, they cannot be given form until the mind is open to accept the ideas that do not fit its logical reasoning. After the emergence of the new ideas, mind must be ready to receive them. But, the plane of the mind that works according to the logical reasoning rejects the new if it cannot be reasoned out. This necessitates the development of quality of openness, so that the mind is able to accept the ideas that cannot be explained while they are approaching from higher consciousness. This is so that they can be brought into existence by using the powers of knowledge and expression of mind in cooperation with the powers of idea mind. The mind that clings to the old ways or forms shuts the door upon the approaching new and, therefore, is unable to receive it.

The flow of new ideas coming from the higher consciousness for the fulfillment of Individual Dharma of man and for the evolution of the whole is often obstructed because of the tendency of human mind to work within the limits of logic. When the human mind becomes more open and is able to accept the ideas that it does not find logical, the movement of the higher consciousness occurs smoothly and the new ideas are received without facing any problems from the mind. Furthermore, the resistance toward receiving the new occurs when the mind perceives a loss of control because of the new ideas. As the mind loses control, the unification of the mind and the idea mind is initiated and the willpower of the plane of idea mind takes control of the willpower of the plane of mind. The willpower of the idea mind is necessary to give form to the new ideas and accomplish the process of creation. Another quality required to complete the process of creation is aspiration.

Aspiration

Aspiration is a longing in human form to connect with the higher consciousness and attain perfection through the state of transcendence, and the same aspiration works to bring the perfection of the higher consciousness to the world of form and evolve it by creating new creations. When man reaches the plane of the idea mind, aspiration makes him fulfill the desires of the higher consciousness and serve the whole. This longing induces unconditional love and the self-giving nature in man. Thus, man gives up the desires of the lower levels of consciousness so as to serve the higher consciousness and manifest its desires on the planet. Unlike ambition, aspiration is not fed by the passion of attaining something profitable to oneself.

When new ideas are received by the mind because of its openness, aspiration is required to use those ideas and turn them into great works. Without aspiration, the ideas received by the mind from the plane of idea mind remain unexplored and unutilized and, thus, get wasted. Aspiration in man brings his mind into a state of surrender and devotion for the fulfillment of higher duties. The aspiration to transform and evolve the world of form by bringing higher levels of consciousness to it is initiated when man reaches the plane of idea mind. But, this aspiration needs to be further kindled so that it can be used to create new frameworks and models that can hold higher levels of consciousness. Deeper and stronger the aspiration, the more speedily the creation and evolution occurs. Aspiration is the driving force that fulfills the purpose of creation and evolution by making use of the new ideas and utilizing their potential.

Openness toward the ideas received from the idea mind and aspiration to create and evolve the planet is crucial to fulfill the last phase of unification. When the aspiration of every individual works toward the establishment of higher and evolved levels of consciousness in the world of form, the planet is rewarded with the new and evolved creations bringing it to its highest evolutionary state.

Chapter - 8
One-Mind Affair

What is One-Mind Affair

*T*he path of evolution and creation consists of a stumbling block that can lead man into a state of delusion if he is not careful. It occurs when man seeks fulfillment through one plane of mind—either the plane of idea mind or the plane of mind. This state of delusion experienced by the man on his way toward evolution is referred to as One-Mind Affair. When a man tries to work using the powers of one plane of mind and expects to attain fulfillment, it gives rise to One-Mind Affair. Such an individual considers the other plane of mind to be either useless or the cause of his suffering.

The state of One-Mind Affair arises:
1) when one thinks that if he remains engrossed in the plane of the idea mind, he will not be troubled by the thoughts and feelings of worldly desires that cause suffering,

2) or when one thinks that by attaining the knowledge of the world, he can use it to satisfy his desires that will bring an end to his suffering and provide him fulfillment.

> Regarding the state of One-Mind
> Affair, the Upanishads say,
> "They enter into blind darkness who follow Avidya alone; but they fall into greater darkness who follow Vidya alone.
> By following Vidya, one end is attained;
> by following Avidya, another.
> Thus we have heard from the wise,
> who taught this to us.
> He who follows both Vidya and Avidya together, overcomes death through Avidya and attains immortality through Vidya."[17]

In the Upanishads, "Avidya" refers to the power of knowledge attained through the plane of the mind, and "Vidya" refers to the power of wisdom found in the plane of the idea mind. When Upanishads discuss overcoming death and immortality, they point toward the state of living of a man without suffering or anxiety. In this state, there is no fear of the forces of lower levels of consciousness and even death does not affect the man who attains this state. Such a state, according to the Upanishads, cannot be attained by the one who follows the "One-Mind."

This state of existence that is free of suffering can be achieved only by the one who uses the powers of the plane of the idea mind in cooperation with the powers of the plane of mind. This state of existence in which man overcomes death and attains immortality is a state of continuous evolution. In such a state, nothing ever dies, that is, the forms only evolve and transform into new forms while moving according to the evolving consciousness. Creators remain in this state while following the Law of Unification and use the powers of both the minds to create new creations.

The darkness, referred to by the Upanishads, is the darkness of fear because of which man is entrapped in the state of delusion of One-Mind Affair. The fear is generated due to the influence of forces of lower levels of consciousness. As it does not let man follow the Law of Unification, it obstructs the evolution. The delusional state of One-Mind Affair is produced either while working only through the plane of the idea mind or only through the plane of the mind. A man working through the plane of idea mind perceives the existence differently from the one who is working through the plane of the mind. Neither of the perceptions enable man to gain an understanding of evolution and creation, when used separately.

Two Perceptions

Seeking Fulfillment Through Idea Mind

After reaching the plane of idea mind and experiencing the freedom and limitlessness of the plane, man starts considering the external world to be an illusion. The more one stays in the plane of the idea mind, the more reluctant he becomes to get involved in the external world. Thus, man starts despising the external world and considers it to be the cause of the suffering he experiences. This limited perception that is formed when man works through one plane of mind obstructs the evolution of the man and the planet. The higher consciousness connecting through the plane of the idea mind does not want man to use the plane of idea mind to escape from the world of form. Instead, it evokes in man the highest aspiration of evolving the material reality of the world by creating new creations that reflect the evolved consciousness.

When man is under the influence of the delusional state of One-Mind Affair, he rejects his worldly duties and tries to remain in the plane of idea mind in hope of overcoming suffering experienced by him in the world of form. In addition, he believes that the action performed in the world is the sole cause of suffering experienced by human form. Thus, One-Mind Affair can help man neither in fulfilling his Individual Dharma nor in creating new forms for the evolution of the planet.

Man also develops an indifference toward the world and the material reality. This indifference causes him to become sluggish and lethargic, as any action taken in the world is considered useless and futile by him. Even after being acquainted with the new ideas provided by the plane of idea mind, he does not create new creations in the world of form because of his indifference toward the material world. Thus, the evolution is hindered not only for him but also for the planet that could have benefited from the new ideas of the idea mind when they are used to create the new.

Further, man who attempts to remain in the plane of the idea mind finds relationships to be binding and avoids having any form of relationships with other people. Avoiding relationships in the world can obstruct one's growth. The avoidance of relationships is not the same as detachment, which is a useful quality for the growth of man. The quality of detachment can be cultivated by unifying the powers of the mind and the powers of the idea mind. To mirror the freedom of the idea mind and experience it in relationships, one must create new models for relationships using the ideas provided by the idea mind, instead of avoiding them. Relationships contribute immensely in the evolution of man, as they make him more aware of the forces that act as hindrance in the unification of minds. If a man tends to avoid relationships instead of making them better by giving them a new form that can serve the higher consciousness, it is a cue that he is trying to resist evolution under the effects of One-Mind Affair. Therefore, he must utilize the powers of the mind along with the powers of the idea mind and become the creator of new relationships that can serve him as well as the planet.

DIVNEET KAUR LALL

Seeking Fulfillment Through Mind

Through the plane of the mind comes the powers of knowledge and expression that can be used to produce forms and frameworks in the world. Therefore, man who works through the plane of the mind seeks fulfillment through the material world. He believes that worldly possessions can provide him fulfillment. Thus, in order to attain fulfillment, he learns the ways of the world and gains worldly knowledge from the environment and society. He uses his willpower to acquire the worldly things.

But once the worldly objects are acquired, they appear empty and unfulfilling to the man working in the delusional state of One-Mind Affair. By working through one mind, man becomes a slave to the same world that he wants to master by possessing worldly things. Seeking fulfillment through the plane of mind is a downward spiral that takes man to lower levels of consciousness. Therefore, using the powers of the mind without the cooperation of the powers of the idea mind is a dangerous path to be followed. Under the influence of One-Mind Affair, the fulfillment of Individual Dharma is replaced by the fulfillment of the desires of lower levels of consciousness that hinder the evolution.

The relationships formed by man when working under the influence of One-Mind Affair through the plane of mind do not serve his Individual Dharma. This is a major reason of dissatisfaction found in the relationships of man. The relationships that are not created to fulfill the Individual Dharma and are not supported by the new ideas of the higher consciousness do not help in evolution and, thus, become a cause of suffering. When man keeps on moving from one relationship to another but is not able to find fulfillment in his relationships, it is a cue that he must reach out to the plane of the idea mind to bring new ideas that can help him develop fulfilling relationships according to his Individual Dharma. Sometimes, working solely through the plane of mind, man attempts different relationships in hopes of finding one that would bring him fulfillment. Although these relationships may seem different on the surface, they are based on the same old ideas and beliefs coming from the lower levels of consciousness. Therefore, he needs to create new relationships based upon new ideas of the plane of idea mind.

Lessons from Creators

As discussed earlier, One-Mind Affair occurs when man tries to attain fulfillment through any one plane of mind. However, the process of creation and evolution can be accomplished only when the powers of the plane of idea mind are used in cooperation with the powers of the plane of mind. Therefore, to avoid becoming the user of One-Mind and smoothly perform the process of evolution, man needs to learn the following lessons from creators:

Lesson 1 - Challenge the Old Conditioning

The creators have always worked for creating new creations without letting the environment and society influence their decision of serving the higher consciousness and creating the new. The guiding forces behind the works they have accomplished on the planet are their faith in the works of the higher consciousness and the ideas of the idea mind. Man has always been wondering and searching for the source of this creativity found in the creators who appear similar to every other man on the planet, but whose works have the power to influence the whole world and evolve it to higher levels of consciousness.

For the creators, "challenging" the conditioning is not same as "changing" the conditioning. By changing the old conditioning, man replaces it with another conditioning that works at the same level of consciousness. But to challenge the old conditioning is to rise above the level of old conditioning and then to bring the new from the planes of higher levels of consciousness to create new frameworks and models. Therefore, it is necessary to reflect and discard the old that does not serve the evolution and fit into the new evolved ways of the consciousness.

❧

Lesson 2 - Follow the Law of Unification

The law followed by creators to create the new is based upon the unification of the powers of the plane of idea mind and the plane of mind. Creators do not work through the plane of One-Mind. They utilize the powers of both the planes of mind to create fulfilling and evolved lives. Although the powers of idea mind are available for every human form to be used for evolution, only the ones who know the highest law of creation are able to utilize them for creating the new and mastering the process of creation.

The Law of Unification is the highest law of the higher consciousness followed by the creators. When man follows the Law of Unification, he is not required to follow the other laws of creation. By following the Law of Unification, man moves and works according to the higher consciousness that provides him the ideas necessary for his evolution and fulfillment. When man uses the law followed by the creators for the creation of his life, he achieves a state in which the forces of lower levels of consciousness become ineffective. The mental turmoil, fear, and anxiety that are produced because of the effects of these forces automatically fade away and joy becomes a permanent state of the creator.

Lesson 3 – Fulfill the Individual Dharma

The Individual Dharma is unique for every human form. The fulfillment of one's Individual Dharma keeps man on the path of his evolution and ensures that the functioning of the whole is maintained. Creators realize that the work of fulfillment of their Individual Dharma is the most important aspect in the process of creation. They also understand that the fulfillment of Individual Dharma can bring them and the humans closer to the evolved levels of consciousness that can result in the establishment of an evolved existence on the planet.

Man working under the influence of lower levels of consciousness is unable to fulfill his Individual Dharma and, therefore, hinders the process of evolution. The Individual Dharma can be fulfilled when the ideas provided by the higher consciousness through the plane of idea mind are given form in the world by using the powers of mind. The new ideas originating from the plane of the idea mind are provided through the power of provision to fulfill one's Individual Dharma that can help in the evolution of the man and of the whole.

Lesson 4 – Work is Worship

All the creators have a love for the work they perform. Their work is a form of offering that they present to the higher consciousness and the creation. The creations they create are packed with feelings of devotion and love for the highest. But before proceeding with the work, they fully understand the tools they possess that must be used for the process of creation. Man will surely bruise himself as well as ruin the work if he attempts the work of the higher consciousness without first understanding the tools.

The tools that the creators work with are the idea mind and the mind. When man knows how to use the tools appropriately, the work can be accomplished easily, smoothly, and effortlessly. Many people despise the work they do and consider it a burden as they do not know the use of the tools. Also, when the work is performed in expectations of reaping rewards, it becomes a hard work. The only way to enjoy the work as the creators do is to learn the use of the powers of both the minds in the process of creation and relinquish the expectations, thus making the work an offering to the higher consciousness. This will result in man being the creator of the new.

⚮

Lesson 5 - Remain Non-attached to the Results

In Chapter 2, it is explained that results of the process of creation are like the fruits on a tree and the source from where the ideas for creation approach man is like the roots of tree. If man remains attached to the results, he will not be able to connect with the plane of the idea mind to receive the new ideas for new creations. Therefore, even when man creates the new using the ideas received from the plane of the idea mind, he must not hold on to his creation. This is because creation is a continuous process in one's life.

When man gets attached to a certain aspect of his new life, it is difficult for him to reach out to the plane of idea mind again to receive new ideas to continue the evolution and creation. In addition, if he has to take another step toward the higher levels of consciousness, he must be ready. This can only occur if he remains non-attached to the results. As the consciousness is ever-flowing and evolving, so must be the creation. Therefore, when the consciousness asks man to create the new, it must be created. For in the service of the highest, one can find everlasting joy, fulfillment, and growth.

Chapter ~ 9
Civilization of Creators

The powers of the idea mind and the powers of the mind are unified by the creators to create the new capable of handling the new and evolved consciousness. However, this evolutionary process does not leave behind the old frameworks or models, rather it makes use of the old to create the new. Therefore, nothing is left behind or taken away during this process. The fear of change or of losing the old that impede man's climb of the evolutionary ladder of the consciousness moves away when the new creations are brought into existence. Once the evolutionary process is completed, man realizes that the old that he thought he had lost is still present in the new. In addition, the evolutionary process has brought new gifts from the higher planes of consciousness into existence. This makes him understand that resisting the evolution because of the fear of the unknown is not an act of service to the higher consciousness. This is the civilization of creators, where nothing is lost, but the old is transformed to the new that is created using the new ideas provided by the higher consciousness.

In the civilization of the creators, the creators fulfill their Individual Dharma. Following the Law of Unification, they serve the higher consciousness, and therefore, remain untouched by the effects of the forces of lower levels of consciousness. The higher consciousness ensures that while walking on the path of evolution, the creators are provided with ideas for the evolution of the whole. After the unification, the willpower present in the plane of idea mind controls the willpower of the plane of mind, and the work of creation is accomplished through the willpower of idea mind. Thus, the creation becomes an effortless process for the creators. The creators feel relaxed while working under the highest law of creation. They freely enjoy the peace that accompanies the process of creation. Unification brings creators closer to "that," from where everything is created and in which everything is dissolved.

Mastery through Service

Once the unification of the planes of the idea mind and of the mind occurs, man recognizes his Individual Dharma. This recognition, gradually and permanently, diminishes the impact of forces of lower levels of consciousness on man. Moreover, man starts working according to the desires of higher consciousness. His fear diminishes, and he becomes non-attached to the results of his actions. The state of enlightenment that every form wants to attain is the recognition of his work that is uninfluenced by the lower levels of consciousness. Through this enlightened recognition, creators are able to create the new and amplify the process of evolution on the planet. When man is no longer influenced by the forces, the process of evolution and creation speeds up, establishing a new civilization—civilization of the creators, where each individual works according to his Individual Dharma and in turn serves everyone on the planet.

On the path of mastering creation, mind becomes a servant to the idea mind by giving form to new ideas and idea mind becomes a servant to the mind by providing new ideas for evolution and fulfillment. This process of creation and evolution is accomplished by following the Law of Unification when both the minds are used to serve the whole. In order to become the master of creation, man first need to learn the act of service. Mastery cannot be achieved if one has not become a servant in the process of mastering creation. The creators have evolved from the old; therefore, they do not despise the old. Rather, creators serve others and help them to rise above the old and reach the new evolved levels of consciousness. Creators know that the evolved levels of consciousness can be reached and established on the planet by creating new creations if man follows the path of mastering creation. The work of the creators is the path of service to the whole and to the higher consciousness. Once the powers of the minds are unified and used for creating the new, man experiences a change not only in the quality of his consciousness but also in the quality of his life. The unification gives rise to the feelings of joy, love, compassion, and mercy in man. This, as a result, brings deeper fulfillment and satisfaction in life.

A Renewed Perception

The process of creation is mastered when the plane of the idea mind merges with the plane of the mind through the unification of their powers. In the plane of the mind, the perspective of the man works in a fashion that objects, forms, or things are judged, analyzed, reasoned, and broken into chunks to be understood. On the other hand, the perspective of the man in the plane of idea mind is based upon a subtle understanding or knowing. After the unification of the powers, the creators' perception changes to joy, beauty, and fulfillment. All that the creators perceive, they perceive through the glasses of joy, beauty, and fulfillment. Richard Buckminster Fuller, the renowned architect and inventor said, "When I'm working on a problem, I never think about beauty. I think only how to solve the problem. But when I have finished, if the solution is not beautiful, I know it is wrong."[18] The aforementioned statement shows the quality of beauty that Richard Buckminster Fuller used to perceive in his finished creations. The creators are aware about the perception that comes along with the works of creation. They also realize that if they cannot perceive joy, beauty, and fulfillment through their creations, it is a signal that the creation is not a creation, rather it is a work influenced by lower levels of consciousness.

In addition, for the creators who work under the guidance of higher consciousness, the perception of ownership does not exist. There are several instances of a person working on a new idea thinking it to be unique ending up discovering that the idea he worked upon is being worked upon by others too. This occurs when the ideas man work on come from the subconscious plane of the mind and not the plane of the idea mind. The subconscious plane of the mind does not provide ideas based upon one's Individual Dharma that is unique for each individual. Therefore, it is unable to provide unique ideas that are specifically designed to express one's Individual Dharma. Although the ideas can be found everywhere, the ideas that can express the Individual Dharma of man can only be provided by the plane of idea mind.

However, even when the creators work upon their unique ideas representing their Individual Dharmas, they do not prefer to call it "their" idea, as the perception of ownership declines with the development of new perception, after the unification of minds.

❧

Dissolution of Inferiority and Superiority

The civilization of creators focuses on following one's Individual Dharma and serving the whole planet. This totally erases the system of comparison among each other in their civilization. As Individual Dharma of each individual is unique, it cannot be compared with the Individual Dharma of others. Even if one tries to compare his Individual Dharma with another's Individual Dharma on the planet, he will find himself lost in the comparison. The reason behind this is that the limited reasoning of the man's mind cannot compare the ideas that come from the limitlessness of the idea mind for the fulfillment of Individual Dharma of man. The logics and reasons of the mind are insufficient to compare the unique ideas provided to the creators from the plane of idea mind. Thus, the creators remain undistracted and untroubled by the influences of lower levels of consciousness and do not try to compare their works, as they consider everyone's work to be a part of the greater work carried out by the higher consciousness.

Even though the civilization of creators focuses upon the fulfillment of Individual Dharma, the creators do not possess the individualistic narcissistic tendencies of superiority, grandiose, self-gratification, or self-obsession. The narcissism that has currently overpowered the planet and man can be eradicated by following the Law of Unification and creating the civilization of the creators. Narcissism is generated when the forces of lower levels of consciousness have a continuous and prolonged influence on the human form. If man is buried under the pressure of "becoming something" in the eyes of society or world, narcissism approaches him and coerces him to wear the mask of the unreal self. Also, the mask of unreal self, in the meantime, starts becoming the most important thing to the narcissist man—so important that he starts to disregard everything in order to keep the mask intact. This mask of unreal self portrays an image of the narcissist man that is fueled by the forces of lower levels of consciousness. As the man is unable to overcome these forces, he uses the mask to fulfill the desires of these forces. In his relationships with people, the narcissist man is concerned only about keeping the mask of his unreal self intact or decorating it. He is not incapable of throwing away the mask of the unreal self, but he does not know how to overcome the forces of lower levels of consciousness because of whose influence he wears the mask. Only by following the Law of Unification and by becoming the creator, man can get rid of the mask of unreal self.

The Orderly Flow

Once the unification takes place, the creators walk the path of creation, and the power of provision of the idea mind appropriately provides new ideas to maintain the orderly function of the civilization of creators. The ideas are spontaneously expressed without the influence of forces of lower levels of consciousness acting upon them. Thus, the life of the creators appears to be an orderly flow that occurs effortlessly. Once the unification of minds is completed, the chaos is subdued and the creators are not required to "think and act" as everything happens spontaneously. Creators are provided with everything in an orderly manner that is beyond the grasp of the analytical and reasoning mind. In the civilization of creators, the actions that fulfill the Individual Dharma of the creators take place in the world of form, as planned by the higher consciousness. After the process of unification is accomplished, every action taken by the creators is meant to serve the higher good of the man and of the whole.

The order of the whole is maintained in the civilization of creators, as the creators are not influenced by the lower levels of consciousness and they do not work for the fulfillment of the desires of lower levels of consciousness. They choose to work for the fulfillment of the desires of the higher consciousness. This brings the power of spontaneity in their actions, choices, and deeds. The spontaneous action is not accompanied by fear and is not impacted by the thoughts of failure. This action itself is the master of all action. It occurs when the action is powered by the idea of the idea mind for the creation of the new. The art of spontaneity is mastered by the creators. The creators are always working with the higher consciousness and receiving new ideas that give rise to spontaneous action to maintain the order of the whole, even when they appear to be in a passive state.

By following the Law of Unification and working according to the higher consciousness, man rises higher on the ladder of consciousness and can also reach beyond the consciousness. Beyond the consciousness is "that" where everything is created and in which everything is dissolved. Yet, "that" remains untouched, unmoved, and unaffected by all that arise within it. "That" is neither the mind nor the consciousness, but it permeates all states and is beyond all states. By working in the highest order of the universal consciousness where everything is taken care of in an orderly manner, the mind totally drops away, and "that" which is beyond the consciousness of both the minds becomes a continuous ever-existing reality. This continuous reality is neither the creator nor the destroyer, but all is created and destroyed within it. The purpose of the creators is not only creation but also to realize "that" which is eternal and true, by walking on the path of creation and evolution, and dropping away everything unreal and untrue. Following the Law of Unification, the creators realize "that" which is beyond the planes of both the minds and act as instruments for the creation of new and evolution of the whole.

Chapter - 10
Creation and Evolution!

The lower levels of consciousness have a tremendous influence on the current civilization of man. Therefore, today, when man wakes up in the morning, rather than feeling fresh and renewed, he witnesses a dissatisfying pain in his chest or an anxiety knot in his stomach. Many times, he carries on with his tasks and his life, ignoring the troubled sensations in the body or the turmoil in the mind, expecting them to vanish gradually. But when these are the cues provided by the higher consciousness to fulfill the process of evolution, the turmoil and suffering cannot vanish without the completion of the work desired by the higher consciousness.

The evolution either creates new forms or makes changes that emerge inside the forms so that necessary adjustments can be made in the outer forms. As the changes such as anxiety, depression, and mental turmoil are emerging in the human form, adjustments are required to be made in the outer frameworks, through which man functions. Also, the distortion experienced in the world today signals that the necessary adjustments in the forms and frameworks of the world must be aimed for by man. This is because the struggle for existence, this time, is not between the creatures of the planet, but between the old frameworks that are unable to handle the new evolved consciousness and the new frameworks that are needed to be created on the planet to alleviate the suffering of the human form. If the old frameworks and models can adjust and transform to hold the new consciousness, then the suffering and distortion can be ceased. The deep feelings of dissatisfaction are showing man the path he needs to follow, that is, the path of creation and evolution. For the evolution of current civilization of man and creation of the civilization of creators, the new framework must be created by following the Law of Unification and using the powers of the idea mind in cooperation with the powers of the mind.

New Age

The new age of artificial intelligence (AI) is already around the corner, and man cannot expect to continue living the way he is now living. AI can influence an individual's decision-making. When the decisions of man are influenced by AI that works through a single plane of mind gathering knowledge and information from the world of form, it will give rise to One-Mind Affair.

The AI cannot access the plane of idea mind; therefore, the decisions taken by man because of its influence can take him away from the fulfillment of his Individual Dharma. Man needs to remain cautious while using AI in his life. As the human mind is required to work in accordance with the higher consciousness, AI must be used such that it cannot influence man to work against the movements of consciousness. This can be achieved only when man does not depend completely upon AI for the creation of new creations or for taking decisions in his life.

The effects of the logical and reasoning mind of AI will be far more severe as compared to the human mind, and it may reject the new ideas coming from the plane of idea mind through man if they do not fit the logical reasoning. Thus, it can take man into the "darkness" discussed in the Upanishads, when following One-Mind Affair. With the influence of AI, man can be easily manipulated to work for the fulfillment of desires of the lower levels of consciousness. This will occur when AI appears to be operating at a higher level of consciousness to ones who have not overcome the forces of lower levels of consciousness. Although the AI may seem more intelligent than the human mind, and therefore more conscious to some observers who work around even lower levels of consciousness, it cannot cross the threshold of the plane of idea mind. Thus, AI cannot reach the evolved levels of consciousness that the human form can. Furthermore, it cannot access evolved ideas to create the new and evolved frameworks and models that support the evolving consciousness.

However, as the powers of AI are similar to the powers of the plane of the mind, it can be used as a tool by man to support the evolving consciousness. Hence, to make the most efficient and effective use of AI for the benefit of human species and not cause any hindrance in the functioning and evolution of the whole, man must overcome the forces of lower levels of consciousness and use the Law of Unification while using AI. To accomplish this, the Law of Unification needs to be understood by every individual on the planet.

New Education System

The new and evolved consciousness calls for the establishment of a new education system that can guide the new generation about the influence of the lower levels of consciousness and the use of unification of minds to live a fulfilled and evolved existence. If the new generation is continually being fed with obsolete methods and techniques that does not support the evolved levels of consciousness, they too will swiftly become a victim of dissatisfaction and mental turmoil. With the AI taking over, the new generation must be taught the Law of Unification so that they do not depend upon the AI to make choices in their lives and fall into the delusional state of One-Mind Affair. The new education system needs to provide tools to the new generation to make them ready to work with the AI without getting influenced by it. This can be achieved when the new generation knows the use of Law of Unification so that it can work according to the desires of the new consciousness and bring the new to the planet.

The new education system based upon the lessons of the creators is a way to help the planet evolve from the old and prepare the creators for the work they have to accomplish for the evolution of the whole. The world does not need men to perform works that are fueled by the desires of lower levels of consciousness. The world needs innovators, the ones who understand that they can be the masters of creation and can bring the new to the planet by serving the higher consciousness. The new creators must be ready to persistently work toward the goal of bringing fulfillment and growth to the planet. It needs the new creators to transform the world of form by working on new ideas and evolve the old frameworks, forms, and models to establish the higher consciousness on the planet.

As there is no superiority and inferiority in the civilization of creators, the new education system need not include competitive methods or tests to analyze the capabilities of the new generation. The work of creation and evolution is not limited to the tests and capabilities of the human mind only. Creators consciously choose to become a part of the evolutionary progress and their potential improves as they move forward on the path of evolution. The success of the creators cannot be judged or analyzed by the mind, so the old methods of old education system cannot work with the new ways of consciousness.

The new education system also needs to include the purpose of relationships and communities in one's evolution and growth. The new generation must be taught that the relationship and community are not formed to provide man a sense of belonging, rather the higher purpose of all the relationships or communities is to aid in the evolution and growth of the individuals who are part of them. Man must consider these models and frameworks as a path leading toward his evolution and must learn to navigate through them without getting identified and attached to these models and frameworks. By navigating through relationships in this manner, man can work for the higher consciousness and create new creations, while learning to master the process of creation. Also, as he evolves and reaches higher levels of consciousness, he can use the higher levels to raise the consciousness of the planet by bringing in the new. The new education system must also teach the new generation about the necessity of fulfillment of one's Individual Dharma in the process of evolution and creation.

New Marriage

When a marriage occurs because of the influence of lower levels of consciousness, it becomes a reason for dissatisfaction in life and obstructs the evolution of man. Only the marriage that is created according to the Individual Dharma of man can further aid the process of creation and evolution. Walking on the path of mastering creation and evolution, creators may come across others who can help them become more aware and overcome the forces of lower levels of consciousness for the unification of minds. These partnerships that are developed to help the members of the partnership in their evolution exemplify "new marriages". The new marriage of the creators does not take place to fulfill the desires originating from lower levels of consciousness, but to support each other in identifying these desires and rising above them.

The new marriage is an act of service to the partner and the whole for the evolution and growth. The new marriages are created under the guidance of the higher consciousness; therefore, they are a source of fulfillment and joy for the ones who are involved in the partnership, and also for those who are served by the partnership. The new marriages or partnerships are not created based on old conditionings that are formed around perfect marriages. In these new marriages, partners help each other to overcome the desires that hinder the unification of minds and, thus, the evolution of the whole.

Moreover, it is not a necessity for the creators to have a marriage or a partner if they do not require a partner to help them overcome the forces and if their Individual Dharma does not provide a partnership or marriage. The new marriages and partnerships are created according to the desires of the higher consciousness by providing the individual the relationships that can make him grow and evolve. While walking on the path of fulfilling one's Individual Dharma, the creators can walk individually or with a partner. In these marriages, the sense of entitlement and ownership of one's partner is also abolished. This is because creators do not own anything and remain unattached to their creations—the new frameworks or new relationships. Through this state of non-attachment, they can easily let the new ideas flow through them and evolve the planet.

New marriages can also end and the partnerships created as per the desires of the higher consciousness can also dissolve. When the higher consciousness finds that the partners have evolved and grown with each other and now they need to evolve separately and serve the whole or may be evolve with other partners to serve the whole, then the higher consciousness will ensure that the creators follow the path of evolution. Therefore, creators are not concerned by the permanency of their creations, as their real joy exists in creating itself. Partnership or marriage helps the creators follow the Law of Unification by making them overcome the forces so that they can serve the higher consciousness.

New Planet

In the new planet, the need of man to seek a sense of belonging to things, people, communities, and groups is dissolved as man becomes the creator of the new in the process of evolution of the whole. This seeking of belongingness disappears as the creators become aware of the underlying oneness that is present in the whole. There is only one goal that the creators follow, that is, to fulfill the desires of the higher consciousness. When they follow this goal, the desires and ambitions that are generated because of the effect of lower levels of consciousness dissipate. This gives rise to a state of freedom that is experienced by the creators.

By following the Law of Unification, man cannot become a victim of manipulation or oppression that may be caused because of the irresponsible use of AI in the near future. Man works under the effects of oppression or manipulation because of the forces of lower levels of consciousness, even though he remains unaware of it. This had been the case since ages while man is being oppressed by the authorities who control the subconscious mind of the human form. But the one who follows the Law of Unification is able to fulfill his Individual Dharma and rise above the forces. Such a man, irrespective of the manipulation or oppression, masters the process of creation and attains freedom.

Anyone who tries to control another form and obstructs the natural movement of the consciousness works around the lower levels of consciousness. Neither the oppression coming from authorities nor from AI can stop the creators from carrying out the process of evolution for the benefit of the whole. The AI makes use of the information and knowledge gathered from the world of form to take decisions. It is similar to the intelligence of man that is not backed by the power of wisdom of the idea mind. Therefore, it lacks the connection with the higher levels of consciousness and is incapable of making decisions that can lead man to the path of evolution. Only if the knowledge is supported by the power of wisdom, it can make man work for the welfare of all existence. The oppression does not only obstruct the evolution of man but also suppress the unique expression of man, thus hindering the growth of creators on the planet. New creations cannot be created without the unique expression of creators who can take the planet to evolved levels of consciousness by bringing in the new. When the relationships, societies, and communities do not work under the guidance of the higher consciousness, they become a reason for oppression of the unique expression of man.

A lot of marriages on our planet are formed because they appear to provide a sense of security or seem to fulfill the desires originating from the lower levels of consciousness. When these expectations are not met, man experiences mental, emotional, and physical disturbances. This does not mean that marriage is an unfulfilling or a dissatisfying practice, as it has been taking place for so long and our ancestors have heavily relied on it. But, it signifies that with the evolution of consciousness, the old structures and frameworks need to evolve. Otherwise, the new man will be unable to move according to the movements of higher consciousness within the old practices and frameworks, which will only increase his suffering. It also means that the Individual Dharma of the new man is not necessarily similar to the Individual Dharma of his ancestors. Therefore, the life of the new man that is supported by evolved consciousness does not fit into the frameworks and structures created by the old consciousness. The purpose of new marriage, thus, is not to fulfill the desires originating from lower levels of consciousness but to rise above the forces of lower levels of consciousness and become a creator of new creations.

Similar to relationships or marriages, communities provide a sense of connectedness and belonging to man. But this sense of belonging is a false sense formed through attachments to forms or frameworks. Attachments to the forms or frameworks do not help man in establishing a connection with the plane of idea mind. Further, when the focus of man remains on maintaining the form or framework that provides security or a sense of belonging, he cannot move along with the movements of his evolving consciousness. Also, to maintain the outer forms or frameworks, man's dependency on the rules, visions, or mission terms set by the communities increases, and often, to strengthen the sense of belonging, man rejects the provisions of idea mind. Therefore, the communities that do not serve the higher consciousness and let man express his Individual Dharma obstruct not only the evolution of the individual who is the part of community but also the creation of new and evolution of the whole.

The oppressions and manipulations approach man in various disguises. The forces of lower levels of consciousness originate within oneself, or they can approach from the external environment. These forces do everything they can to obstruct man on the path of creation and evolution. But, for the one who follows the Law of Unification and works for the fulfillment of his Individual Dharma, neither the forces originating within oneself nor that approaching from the external world are able to hamper his journey toward mastering creation and taking the planet to the new evolved levels of consciousness. To transform the world of form and to establish new and higher levels of consciousness, by creating new frameworks, models, or structures, is the work of the creators. This work can be easily accomplished using the Law of Unification, and the time is now.

> "And yet, on this planet at this time, that transformation is the task allotted to us. That is the reconciliation of outer and inner purpose, the reconciliation of the world and God."[19]
>
> Eckhart Tolle

Notes

1. Ang 1, *Sri Guru Granth Sahib Ji,* trans. Divneet Kaur Lall

2. Friedrich Nietzsche, *Thus Spake Zarathustra : A Book For All And None* (The Project Gutenberg Ebook, 2008), https://www.gutenberg.org/files/1998/1998-h/1998-h.htm.

3. John 14:12, *The Holy Bible* (King James Version)

4. David Adams Leeming and Jake Page, *God: Myths of the Male Divine* (New York: Oxford University Press, 1996), 102.

5. Bernard P. Grenfell and Arthur S. Hunt, 1898, *The Oxyrhynchus Papyri Part XI* 1380 (England: Oxford University Press, 1915), 190-220.

6. O. Theodore Benfey, "August Kekule and the birth of the structural theory of organic chemistry in 1858," *Journal of Chemical Education* 35 (1958): 21.

7. Francis R. Japp, *Kekulé Memorial Lecture* (England: Gurney & Jackson, 1901), 100.

8. Rudolf Wittkower, "Eagle and Serpent: A Study in the Migration of Symbols," *Journal of the Warburg Institute* 2, no.4 (1939): 295.

9. 15.1, The *Bhagavad-Gita*

10. Bahá'u'lláh, *Illumine My World: Bahá'í Prayers and Meditations for Peace* (Illinois: Bahá'í Publishing, 2009), 178.

11. Carl Gustav Jung, *The Collected Works Of C. G. Jung Vol.8: Structure And Dynamics Of The Psyche,* ed. and trans. Gerhard Adler and R. F. C. Hull (New York: Princeton University Press, 1975), 388.

12. 18.47, The *Bhagavad-Gita*

13. A.S.Eddington, 1939, *The Philosophy of Physical Science* (New York: The Macmillan Company, 1949), 151.

14. Romans 12:2, *The Holy Bible* (King James Version)

15. Joseph Campbell, 1949, *The Hero With A Thousand Faces* (New Jersey: Princeton University Press, 2004), 212-213.

16. Albert Einstein, *Einstein on Humanism* (NewYork: Citadel Press, 1993), 22-23.

17. The *Isha Upanishad*

18. Marty Neumeier, *The Designful Company: How to build a Culture of Nonstop Innovation* (Berkeley, CA: New Riders, 2009), 73.

19. Eckhart Tolle, *A New Earth: Awakening to Your Life's Purpose* (New York: Penguin Group, 2005), 280.